MoviePlus X3
User Guide

How to Contact Us

Our main office
(UK, Europe):

The Software Centre
PO Box 2000, Nottingham,
NG11 7GW, UK

Main:

(0115) 914 2000

Registration (UK only):

(0800) 376 1989

Sales (UK only):

(0800) 376 7070

Customer Service/
Technical Support:

http://www.serif.com/support

General Fax:

(0115) 914 2020

North American office
(USA, Canada):

The Software Center
13 Columbia Drive, Suite 5,
Amherst NH 03031, USA

Main:

(603) 889-8650

Registration:

(800) 794-6876

Sales:

(800) 55-SERIF or 557-3743

Customer Service/
Technical Support:

http://www.serif.com/support

General Fax:

(603) 889-1127

Online

Visit us on the Web at:

http://www.serif.com/

International

Please contact your local distributor/dealer. For further details, please contact
us at one of our phone numbers above.

Contents

Contents

8. Exporting 181

9. Index 205

Welcome to MoviePlus X3!

Welcome to **MoviePlus X3**, the powerful video-editing program fully certified for Windows® Vista and XP. MoviePlus is the program of choice for video editors looking for easy and intuitive ways to create and share their own movies.

MoviePlus X3 offers an exciting experience at all the key steps of movie creation—from importing media, media management (trimming and scene detection), video editing via storyboard or timeline (for ease-of-use vs. power), through to exporting your project to YouTube, DVD, file, iPod, or PSP.

In this latest release, the new **Storyboard mode** (p. 47) offers a new approach to MoviePlus video editing. Ideal for simpler projects, this mode lets you:

- **Sequence** your clips along a storyboard one-by-one.

- **Change clip order** by drag and drop individually, or as multiple selections.

- Apply stylish **titles**, **captions** and **credits** as text clips, or as overlaid text ("floating" over your video). Apply fantastic animated effects to your text via an Animations gallery.

- **Resize clips** to remove unwanted borders or areas of your video or image.

- **Pan and zoom** for "slideshow" image montages ("Ken Burns effect").

- Introduce **transitions** between clips automatically, and swap out at any time.

- Apply cool special **effects**.

- Use the How To pane for always-at-hand assistance when you need to perform a storyboard task.

Before moving on, you'll be pleased to hear that MoviePlus's award-winning multi-track **timeline** remains as powerful and versatile as ever. Arrange video and audio clips along a chronological timeline, while working with an unlimited number of video and audio tracks (or groups) for a traditional "layers-based" approach! Simply **Switch to Timeline mode** to unleash the tiger in MoviePlus!

Whichever mode you plan to work in, you'll be the envy of your audience at your movie's first screening.

Let's look at the other new features of MoviePlus X3, and the established features that have made MoviePlus so popular with so many budding movie directors.

What's new?

Ease of use

- **Fantastic new look!** (p. 21)
  MoviePlus sports a new contemporary appearance that will make your video editing experience that much more enjoyable.

- **Easy-to-use Panes** (p. 21)
  Enjoy larger and more intuitive panes which can float and be resized—design your own MoviePlus workspace! Make use of full screen previews on additional monitors.

- **Editing Toolbars for More Efficiency**
  Context-sensitive toolbars for storyboard and timeline; toolbars only offer the tools you need, when you need them.

- **Switch Editing Modes**
  Swap between the simplicity of the new storyboard and the power of the timeline. A single click gives an easy jump between either mode.

○ **Edit Multiple Attributes**

Change individual, specific, or all attributes (e.g. transitions, clip durations) at the same time.

Gathering and managing media

○ **Download Media** (p. 27)

Download from **HDD/DVD camcorder** (**AVC HD support**), **USB mass storage devices** (**hard drive**, **memory stick/card**, **flash drives**), or **CD/DVD**. MoviePlus transfers media files straight from your device, ready for use in your Media pane. Media can be saved to a chosen destination.

○ **Quick Sourcing of Video, Audio, Image Content** (p. 27)

Capture video and audio directly from sources like a DV (digital video) camcorder and video capture card. Take images straight off your camera.

○ **Automatic Scene Detection and Management** (p. 35)

Detect and utilize scenes within movies from tape-based camcorders (even adjust detection sensitivity). Exclude unwanted scenes, merge scenes together, or even add manual cuts to trim and split scenes to your liking! The original file is left intact, not split into pieces by the process.

○ **Media Pane** (p. 29)

Your project's media (video, image, and audio files) can be gathered together in a Media pane before commitment to your storyboard (or timeline). For media-rich projects, you can organize media content into folders or even reuse media in subsequent projects by adding to the pane's Library tab. Fix incorrectly oriented image and video files by one-click rotation.

Performance

● **Pre-Rendering for improved video playback**
Render transitions, video clips, or a time range in the background for improved preview performance; lightning fast previews for complex timelines and clips with multiple processor-intensive effects!

Audio

● **Narration Recording** (p. 161)
Record voice-overs while you play back your movie—simply set up your microphone, press record and begin talking!

● **Digital CD Ripping** (p. 164)
Rip your audio CDs—great for creating movie soundtracks from your favourite songs.

● **Dolby® Digital Stereo Support** (p. 184)
For DVD export, MoviePlus now uses Dolby Digital to encode and compress audio (leaving more room for video!). Video files with Dolby Digital streams can also import without the need for third party codecs.

● **Audio Effects** (p. 147)
Choose from a range of audio special effects—Reverb, Bass, Fill Left, Fill Right channel-related effects. Even use third-party VST effect plug-ins.

Text

- **In-Place Text Editing** (p. 169)
  Edit titles, captions, and credits directly on the Video Preview pane for accurate text design and representation. Drag multiple text objects to position text independently of each other.

- **Text Styles** (p. 176)
  For titles, captions, and credits, the new Text Styles gallery offers hand-picked styles for that professional look. Apply a full range of character formatting for custom text styles.

- **Text Animation** (p. 178)
  Bring text to life by choosing In and/or Out animations, all from the new Galleries pane. Fly, Spin, Blinds, Explode, and Type are among an impressive collection of preset categories.

Exporting

- **Even Easier Exporting** (p. 183)
  Export to any media, file or device using either **Basic** or **Advanced** mode—the former uses unchanged project settings, the latter lets you modify project settings for export in a custom export template, which can be saved.

- **Share Worldwide with YouTube** (p. 201)
  Export your movie then automatically upload to your YouTube account.

- **PSP/iPod Export** (p. 198)
  Export mp4 movies to play on these popular devices. Upload to PSP directly from MoviePlus; import movie into iTunes for later syncing with iPod.

⬤ **DVD Menu Designer** (p. 187)

For handy chapter navigation, the **Menu Designer** lets you create your very own menu designs from a diverse range of pre-built templates, by changing layout, background images/music, titling, and button styles. The designer now offers DVD **Preview** (with remote control simulator), video menu backgrounds, and manual positioning of menu buttons. For multi-page menus, each page can adopt its own appearance (e.g., layout, background, etc). Options let you **play your first chapter** before menu displays and create **text-only menus**.

Other improvements

⬤ **Video effects** now include **Old Film**, **Motion Blur**, **Noise**, with a **Chroma Key** effect that inverts. Share your movies much more easily with basic export settings. Filter effects now include **Outlines**, **Blur**, and a **3D Reflection Map** effect. Now **archive to HDV camcorder**. **Menuless DVDs** let you play your movies directly. **Create ISO disc images** for DVDs and VCDs—write using any disc authoring software.

Established features

⬤ **Trimming**

Trim video clips to your preferred length in a dedicated **Trimming** dialog, without affecting your original video clip.

⬤ **Audio Levels**

Avoid audio distortion with the Levels pane—audio level meters indicate if your current audio levels hit the Red. Use as a master control volume to normalize project audio levels prior to movie export. Audio waveforms for any audio clip are optionally displayed on the timeline to help synchronize audio events.

- **Cool Transitions**

  Automatic transitions between two clips make MoviePlus a breeze. MoviePlus offers dozens of built-in, customizable transitions... enjoy standards like wipes and cross-fades through to stretches, pushes, pixellation, and 3D transitions.

- **Computer Generated (CG) clips**

  For movie interludes or backdrops to titles or credits, add coloured **Backgrounds** (solid or gradient fills) or **QuickShapes** such as hearts, chevrons, teardrops, and zigzags (plus many more). QuickShapes are great for masking effects!

- **Stunning Effects**

  Enhance your movies with a wide range of customizable correction filters and special effects. Correction filters include basic brightness, contrast, gamma adjustments, sharpen... and many more! Special effects such as **Shadow**, **Glow**, **Bevel**, **Emboss**, **Colour Fill**, Outlines, Reflections, and **Feathering**, as well as **3D lighting** and **surface effects** are supported. Apply individually or cumulatively.

- **Keyframe Controls**

  Transitions, effects, video motion, opacity, plus audio volume and stereo panning are all "key-framable". You can specify changes over time and all the in-between steps are calculated for you. The changes themselves can also adopt different speeds or accelerations by changing the keyframe properties.

- **Preset Envelopes**

  Use MoviePlus's advanced keyframe technology is even more accessible through a comprehensive new range of preset envelopes— these can be simply dragged and dropped onto video and audio tracks and will perform previously complex video editing techniques, such as opacity, transform and crop, with ease.

Transparent Overlays

All of MoviePlus's video tracks support video transparency to superimpose not just titles but any 32-bit transparent image (or video) over your movie's action. Make portions of existing video transparent by adding a mask (as you might in a bitmap-editing program like Serif PhotoPlus) or by picking a solid colour to become transparent.

Multiple Picture-in-Picture

Create professional picture-in-picture effects using video clips or still frames... Easily edit the size and position of your video in the Video Preview pane. Perfect for showing supplemental visuals without detracting from the main movie, or tiling multiple videos together for a dynamic scene.

Built-in DVD Authoring!

Now bring your movies to the masses with quick and easy authoring to DVD or VCD (includes auto-erase)!

Don't forget to register your new copy, using the **Registration Wizard** on the Help menu. That way, we can keep you informed of new developments and future upgrades!

Licensed feature unlocking

After a fixed time period, you may have to unlock features as part of the MoviePlus import or export process—this is purely for Serif licensing reasons and does not incur any charge. Once unlocked, the feature will be freely available and you will not need to unlock the MoviePlus X3 feature again on your computer.

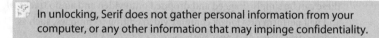

In unlocking, Serif does not gather personal information from your computer, or any other information that may impinge confidentiality.

To unlock features, you will need to connect your computer to the Internet.

Installation

System requirements

Minimum

- Intel® Pentium® II or AMD Athlon™ XP processor

- 256MB RAM

- 382MB free hard drive space (2-5GB of additional space may be required during the composition and export of video projects)

- Graphics card and monitor capable of 800x600 display size and 24-bit colour depth

- Windows-compatible sound controller

- CD-ROM/DVD-ROM drive (for program install)

- Microsoft Windows® XP or Vista

- Microsoft DirectX 9.0b device drivers (included with install)

- Microsoft Windows Media Video support files (included with install)

- An Internet account and connection (for Auto Update and Licensed Feature Unlocking)

Recommended

- Intel® Pentium® 4 Hyper-Threaded processor or Multi-core processor

- 512MB RAM (ideally ≥1GB)

- Fast hard disk (7200rpm drive with dedicated ATA133 connection or better)

- Modern graphics card and monitor capable of 1024x768 display size (ideally 1280x1024)

In addition to the typical processing, disk, and graphics requirements, there are some optional items that may enhance your use of MoviePlus.

Optional

- FireWire (IEEE1394) support for connecting tape-based camcorders

- Video capture card for digitizing and editing analogue video clips

- Windows XP Service Pack 2 (for HDV video capture)

- DVD±R or CD-R drive for Disc writing

- Apple QuickTime software (included with MoviePlus install; up to 156MB)

First-time install

To install Serif MoviePlus X3, simply insert the Program CD into your DVD/CD drive. If AutoPlay is enabled on the drive, this automatically starts the Setup Wizard. If you are installing MoviePlus on Microsoft Windows® Vista, you may need to click on **Run autorun.exe** from within the **Autoplay** dialog. If AutoPlay is not enabled (or doesn't start the install automatically), use the Manual install method described below.

1. The Setup Wizard begins with a **Welcome** dialog, click **Next**>.

2. To add customer information, enter your **User Name**, **Organization** (if applicable), and the software **Product Key** that either came with your software (on your CD's case) or was previously emailed to you. For more information, click the [?]. Click **Next**>.

3. Please read through the scrollable license agreement, then if you agree to the terms, enable the **I Accept...** button. Click **Next**>.

4. You'll need to choose a Default Video Standard. Set this broadcasting and recording standard according to the region in which you intend to share your movie—**NTSC** (North and South American continents, Japan and South Korea) or **PAL** (Europe, Africa, Middle East, Asia, and Oceania). All new MoviePlus projects will adopt this standard by default. Click **Next**>.

5. (Optional) Install QuickTime if you intend to use mov files in MoviePlus. Click **Next**>.

6. In the **Setup Options** dialog, you have the opportunity to customize your installation.

    To install the recommended options, simply click **Next**. However, if you are concerned about disk space, you may choose to run some of the features from the DVD/CD. The drop-down boxes display the available options for each feature:

○   **Will be installed on the local hard drive.** If this option is selected, it will install the feature to your hard disk but will not automatically install any subfeatures that may be available.

○   **Entire feature will be installed on the local hard drive.** By selecting this option, all of the subfeatures relating to this feature will also be installed. Some subfeatures can require a substantial amount of hard disk space.

○ ⊕ **Will be installed to run from the CD.** If this option is selected, you will save space on your hard disk but you will need to have the installation media at hand to access the features.

○ ⊗ **Entire feature will be installed to run from the CD.** This option will allow you to access the content and all of its subfeatures from the installation media, saving you disk space.

○ 🏢 **Will be installed to run from network.** If you are installing the software from a network, this option will allow you to access the content from the network storage, saving you disk space.

○ 🏢 **Entire feature will be installed to run from network.** If you are installing the software from a network, this option will allow you to access the features and all related subfeatures from the network storage, saving you disk space.

○ ✕ **Entire feature will be unavailable.** By choosing this option, you will not be able to use the selected feature. However, if you later decide that you want to use the feature, you will be able to install it by modifying your installation.

When you select a feature installation option, the information pane on the right of the list will inform you of the amount of hard disk space that the feature needs. Not all installation options are available for all features.

> If disk space is not an issue, you may decide to install the entire program to your hard disk. This can improve performance and you will be able to use all of the features without the need to keep the program disk in your DVD/CD drive.

If you do not want to install the program to its default location, click the **Change...** button. Browse to the folder that you want to install MoviePlus in and click **OK**. Caution should be taken here as changing the default settings may affect subsequent installs of later versions of the software.

Changing the installation defaults may result in some options of the program being unavailable. It is only recommended for advanced users.

7.   At the **Shortcut Options** screen, you can choose to automatically create shortcuts by checking the option boxes. Click **Next>.**

8.   Click **Install** to accept your settings and install the program. The dialog will display a progress bar as the program installs. Once installation is complete, click **Finish** to exit the Setup Wizard.

Your installation is now complete and you can begin using Serif MoviePlus X3!

Manual install

For manual installation, use My Computer (Windows® XP), or Computer (Windows® Vista), to navigate to the DVD/CD drive in which your MoviePlus Program CD is located. Double-click the DVD/CD drive and then double-click **setup.exe** in the displayed folder. If you are installing on Windows® Vista, choose Serif MoviePlus X3 from the warning dialog (optional). Follow the on-screen installation instructions.

Modifying, repairing or removing MoviePlus

To modify, repair or remove the installation:

Microsoft Windows XP:

1.   Click the ![start] button and select **Control Panel** from the Windows Start menu.

2.   Double-click on the **Add/Remove Programs** icon.

3.   Locate and select Serif MoviePlus X3 in the list of installed programs.

4.   Click the **Change** button to make changes to the install via the Setup Wizard.

Microsoft Windows Vista:

1. Click the ⊕ **Start** button and click **Computer**.

2. Click the ▣ Uninstall or change a program button.

3. Locate Serif MoviePlus X3 in the list of installed programs, then select it.

4. Click the **Change** button to make changes to the install via the Setup Wizard.

You can also access this via Programs and Features by clicking **Control Panel** from the Windows **Start** menu (or **Settings>Control Panel** from the "Classic" Windows **Start** menu), clicking **Programs** and then clicking **Programs and Features**.

To change the installed features:

Open the Setup Wizard as described in the previous steps. To change the installation, select the **Modify** option and then click **Next**. From here, you will be able to make changes such as removing some of the program features. Adding additional content may prompt you to insert your original MoviePlus X3 Program CD; removing content may or may not require the CD. See the steps in **First-time install** if you are unsure about any of the options.

Some features, such as fonts, cannot be removed by the Setup Wizard once they have been installed. This is due to the way they are used by other applications. Modifying the installation settings in this case will never free up disk space. Fonts in particular, will even remain if the program is completely uninstalled.

Removing MoviePlus

Open the Setup Wizard, select the **Remove** option and click **Next**. Click **Remove** to completely remove MoviePlus from your computer.

Repairing MoviePlus

On occasion, it may be necessary to repair your installation of MoviePlus. This can happen if system files are overwritten by another program or if they are accidentally deleted.

Open the Setup Wizard and select the **Repair** option and click **Next**. Click **Repair**. The repair process will reinstall all files and registry entries, therefore replacing any missing or incorrectly overwritten files. Once the repair has completed, open MoviePlus.

Getting
Started

Visual reference

Standard toolbar · Tasks toolbar · Menu Bar · How to Pane · Video Preview Pane · Media Pane · Galleries Pane · Status Bar · Storyboard toolbar · Timeline toolbar · Context toolbar · Timeline · Storyboard · Properties Pane

Menu bar

The Menu bar in MoviePlus offers a typical range of drop-down menu commands; some are standard to most programs, such as File>New, File>Open, File>Save, Edit>Undo and so on, and some commands are of course specific to MoviePlus functionality, such as Insert>Video Track or Tools>Capture. Hover over any option and read its description on the Status Bar for assistance.

Standard toolbar

Provides a typical range of standard editing tools, typically creating new or opening existing projects, as well as cutting, pasting, and undo/redo operations.

Tasks toolbar

Offers access to the Menu Designer (for menu-driven DVDs/VCDs) and a range of movie exporting options (to disc, camera, file, iPod, PSP, or YouTube).

Storyboard/Timeline toolbars

These toolbars host essential btools for video editing in Storyboard or Timeline mode, respectively. A context toolbar alongside either toolbar offers tools relevant to the currently selected object type (clip, transition, etc.).

How To pane

Shows step-by-step instructions for making and exporting movies in Storyboard mode.

Video Preview pane

Displays your current project, with built-in project playback control and a host of viewing tools.

Media pane

Stores and arranges media files that you've imported, downloaded, captured, and ripped, before dragging to the storyboard (or timeline).

Properties pane

Use the pane to display and modify the properties of any currently selected object (clip, transition, effect, etc.).

Galleries pane

Use the pane to apply transitions, video effects, and text animations by drag-and-drop of presets. Audio effect and envelope presets show in Timeline mode.

Storyboard
The default editing workspace for MoviePlus, the storyboard can be used to add and arrange all video, image, or audio clips along a simple time-based strip. Apply transitions, effects, and add narration.

Timeline
A more advanced workspace based on a traditional video editing timeline; clips can be arranged on "layered" tracks for blending, mixing, and other more complex editing techniques such as masking, overlays, and transforms.

Status bar
Displays helpful, context-sensitive messages about MoviePlus interface elements, as well as status information for selected operations.

Starting a new project

The Startup Wizard

The MoviePlus Startup Wizard offers easy access to the most common
starting tasks after you launch MoviePlus (or when you click **File>New**), i.e.

- **Start New Project** (create a new project; check **Widescreen** if needed)

- **Open Saved Project** (to browse your PC for previously saved
  MoviePlus projects)

- **Browse Tutorials** (learn all about MoviePlus with PDF tutorials)

The Startup Wizard is displayed by default when you launch MoviePlus. If
you don't want to use the Startup Wizard again, check the "Don't show this
wizard again" box. You can switch it on again via the **Use Startup Wizard**
check box in **Tools>Options...** (General tab).

Click the ▧ **Cancel** button or press **Escape** on your keyboard to bypass the Startup Wizard and launch MoviePlus with an empty project. The type of project will match the last project you selected. By default, MoviePlus will be launched in Storyboard mode (see p. 47), an easy-to-use workspace for simpler projects.

MoviePlus projects

MoviePlus bases its movie compositions around "projects". You can save and reopen your projects at any time for ongoing editing. A MoviePlus project file is a collection of project settings (the video size and shape, audio properties, aspect ratio, etc.) plus information about how all your clips are arranged and edited on the timeline. Custom project templates can also be created from any template preset.

To start a new project from the Startup Wizard:

- ○ From the Startup Wizard, select **Start New Project**. MoviePlus automatically picks a DVD project setting with the video standard (PAL or NTSC) set according to your installation.

MoviePlus lets you review and possibly adopt different project settings if necessary.

To use a different project setting:

1. Select **Project Settings...** from the **File** menu.

2. Pick a different project template preset. Templates include DV presets (for maintaining DV movie quality) and DVD presets (for projects intended to create TV- or computer-ready DVDs). Some of these formats offer NTSC/PAL choices for you to choose depending on your local standard, and a Widescreen variant in each case.

3. Click the **OK** button to save your changes.

You can modify the current project settings at any time by modifying its template.

To create a custom project template:

1. Select **Project Settings...** from the **File** menu.

2. From the **Project Settings** dialog, pick a template in the **Templates** list on which to base your new project settings (or select the Multimedia preset for general use).

3. Click the **Modify** button to make a copy of the project, now named (**Untitled**).

    Change various settings including the pixel size of your project, the **Pixel aspect ratio** (many types of output use stretched pixels), the video **Frame rate** (number of frames per second), **Interlacing**, and **Audio sampling rate**.

4. When you are happy with your settings you can save your project template for reuse—simply click the **Save** button, type a new preset name and click **OK**.

Adding media files to your project

The media files you use for your project could reside on a variety of devices, typically on your HDD camcorder's hard disk, DVD camcorder's internal DVD drive, camcorder tape, digital camera, but also on any computer drive (local, network, or DVD/CD). Adding media files simply involves importing, downloading, capturing, or ripping media files into MoviePlus's Media pane.

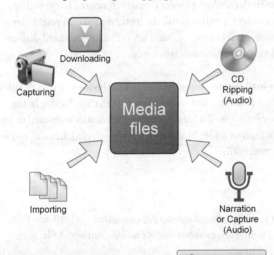

Media files are added by clicking the ![Add Media...] button at the top of the Media pane. The flyout lets you:

Import A standard dialog lets you navigate to, then select one or more media files from **local disk** or **network drive** for import directly into your Media pane. Use **Shift**-select or **Ctrl**-select for adjacent or non-adjacent multiple selection before download.

Download Download media from your **HDD/DVD camcorder**, **USB Hard drive**, **USB memory stick**, **memory card reader**, or **CD/DVD**. For HDD/DVD camcorders, adding media is easier compared to capturing video from camcorder tape (this is still the method used on present-day lower-specification camcorders, e.g. Mini DV). The device's hard disk or DVD is treated as a removable storage device.

From the **Download** button, select the connected **Device** as a remote drive in the dialog, then **Browse...** to a chosen folder, then click **Next>**. In the next screen, the device's media files can be selected and downloaded to your computer's **Destination** folder by clicking **Finish**. Selected files show in the Media pane automatically.

Capture With your tape-based camcorder connected via USB/FireWire you can capture your movie's video footage and/or audio to a file, with optional scene splitting.

Rip CD Rip audio tracks from your favourite audio CDs straight into the Media pane.

The Media pane

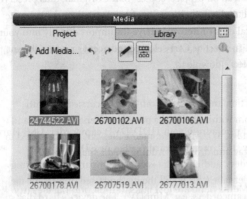

An important function of the Media pane is to manage your media files
before committing media to your storyboard or timeline. In particular, you
can reorder files by clicking and dragging a thumbnail (or selection of) into
the position you wish it to appear on the storyboard (or timeline).

You can fix incorrectly oriented images or movies obtained from your
digital camera by using the **Rotate Left** and **Rotate Right** buttons. Media
files can also be copied, renamed, or removed from your project within the
Media pane by right-click.

Remember that MoviePlus does not perform these operations on your original media, but instead on project "copies" of the original, thus preserving your valuable original media in their original file locations.

 Hover over any media file to view its media properties, and if a video file, a preview of the video.

 Scene detection and trimming can then be carried out with respective buttons from within the Media pane (see Scene Detection and Trimming on p. 35 and p. 37). After that, media files can then be added to your storyboard by drag and drop. See Adding media files on p. 50.

Thumbnails in the Media pane are just links to their original files (try right-click **Properties...** to view file location). As a result, changes made to files within MoviePlus will not affect the originals.

Adding files to your library

If you want to reuse media files in other MoviePlus projects you can save them to your library. Simply right-click the media file and choose **Add to Library**. The view changes to **Library** view where you'll see the file stored in the library's root folder. You can create your own folder structure by selecting **New Folder** on right-click (you can also create folders under the default Projects tab!). You'll also see some resources such as titles, backgrounds, credits, and some tutorial workspace files.

To return to your current project, click the | Project | tab.

To revisit your library at any time (even when using new projects), click the | Library | tab.

Capturing video

MoviePlus makes it easy to **capture** your own video and audio footage to your PC from tape-based digital camcorders (e.g., Mini DV, HDV), analogue video sources (e.g., analogue camcorders, VHS, or TV; all via a capture card) or USB web cams.

Remember that videos stored on tapeless camcorders can be downloaded directly from the device's hard disk or internal DVD. See Adding media files to your project on p. 27.

To set up and initiate the video capture, a Capture Video dialog is used.

This example shows in-progress capture of digital video footage with associated audio from a tape-based camcorder. As you capture (by pressing the **Record** button), the footage is written to a file(s), which shows directly within the Media pane.

To launch the Capture Video dialog:

1. Click the button on the Media pane.

2. From the flyout, select the **Capture** button

OR

- Choose **Capture...** from the **Tools** menu.

To connect your camcorder or other capture device:

If your camcorder is properly connected and supported (and is set to playback mode rather than record mode if appropriate), you should see a video preview in the preview window of the Capture Video dialog when your camcorder is playing.

If you are using an analogue video source, ensure that it is connected to your video capture device (or a USB socket in the case of a web cam).

To choose an appropriate capture format:

If your source footage is on a tape-based camcorder, the video and audio capture settings are greyed out in the **Source Properties** button as the capture format is fixed to the camcorder's format. However, if your source footage is being captured via a video capture device or USB web cam, you can choose a file format suited to your video type by choosing this button.

It is recommended that you capture at a resolution and quality as high as possible to achieve high quality results—it is best to aim as high as the source footage resolution and quality. Even when you ultimately aim for your resulting video to be very compact, for instance to make it suitable for download from the Internet, you can defer the file-size-smashing resizing and compression operations to final export time, don't compromise your captured quality!

To set a suitable file storage location:

Captured video footage can occupy a large amount of hard drive space when it is transferred to your PC, so it is important to choose a drive location with lots of roo.

  Choose **Options>Folders** from the **Tools** menu, then **Browse...** for a different **Capture folder**.

> During capture, you can define a different destination **Folder** within the Capture Video dialog (Output section).

To preview and cue your video footage:

For tape-based camcorders, "navigation" controls under the preview window allow you to cue your tape to the point at which you would like capture to start. For other sources you'll need to control the device yourself, a remote control may be handy here.

To capture with scene splitting:

For DV video, the **Split files by scene** check box offers the chance for all your scenes to be saved as separate video files as part of the capture process. For capture from tape-based camcorder, the default is for the box to be checked so that scenes are split (by timestamp) where the recording has been stopped and restarted; for all other captures, if the box is unchecked, no splitting occurs so you'll capture a single video file.

For non-DV video, e.g. from analogue devices, scene splitting is not possible; the option is unavailable (greyed out) as time stamps are not present. Instead, scene detection can be carried out in the Media pane (see Scene Detection on p. 35). Scene detection does not create separate video files but creates "virtual" scenes from a single video file. Incidentally, you can still use timestamp-based scene detection on DV sources within the Media pane.

For HDV video, scene splitting may not be possible—if so, the **Split file by scene** button will be greyed out.

Record

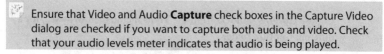 Ensure that Video and Audio **Capture** check boxes in the Capture Video dialog are checked if you want to capture both audio and video. Check that your audio levels meter indicates that audio is being played.

1. Play your video source from at least a couple of seconds before the point at which you'd like capture to start (to allow the video device to begin playing smoothly), then press the [>] button.

2. Click the [Record] button in this dialog to begin the capture.

3. To skip footage, press the [Stop] button to finish capture, then pause the playback by clicking the [>"] button, cue the tape to the point you would like to proceed from, then play and record again to resume the capture.

 Don't use the "navigation" playback controls while recording!

It's better to capture too much footage rather than too little, it can always be trimmed later, so don't worry too much about exactly how much is captured if you are uncertain.

4. When you are happy that all the required footage has been captured, click the **Stop** button, then the **Close** button.

 The captured video footage will show in your Media pane (see p. 29) automatically on closing the Capture Video dialog. The files are still physically located in your Capture Folder.

When MoviePlus captures your video or audio footage with scene detection, it will automatically name and incrementally number your files if you do not specify a particular filename (by default the Prefix "Capture" is used; the number is added as a suffix). To change the prefix name, enter a new name in the dialog's **Prefix** option.

Scene detection

For any video file, scene detection can be carried out in the Media pane at any time. Your original video file is not affected by this process because the clips generated are "virtual scenes"; they are real clips that you can drag straight on to your timeline, but they are merely references to the original video file with separately stored information about where each scene begins and ends. Even if your video file is moved or renamed, once the scenes have been generated, MoviePlus will be able to show you the detected scenes for your media.

DV video files are normally **split** at capture (see p. 31) to create a separate video file per scene. However, non-DV video files such as those from analogue devices cannot be split in this way so benefit from this virtual scene detection method.

 If you're using an HDD or DVD camcorder, you won't need to split or detect scenes. Each scene is stored as an individual video file which can be downloaded to your computer; the files show in your Media pane automatically.

How does it work? MoviePlus detects scenes by firstly searching for any timestamps in the file (if DV video) and, if they're not present, will search for discontinuity between frames. If one frame is very different from its previous frame (based on changes to their colour histograms) it is likely to be considered to be in a separate scene and a scene break is made.

Detection and management of scenes is carried out in a Scenes dialog, which displays a Scenes timeline hosting all of your automatically detected scenes. You can exclude unwanted scenes, merge scenes together, and add your own cuts to create further scenes—just like on a real studio's cutting room floor.

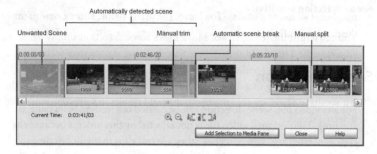

To detect scenes:

1. In the Media pane, select a clip and click the ⊞ **Scenes** button (or right-click the video file and select **Scenes...**).

2. From the **Scenes** dialog, a series of consecutive scenes are detected and displayed along the Scenes timeline. By default, all automatically detected scenes are included. Several operations are possible:

   ● To exclude an unwanted scene, click on it to turn it grey.

   ● To merge scenes together, click the grey dividing line between scenes (it turns green), then choose the **Delete Split** button.

   ● To add your own cut, set the current time indicator to a frame in a scene. If removing footage before the frame, click the **Set In Point** button; to remove footage after the frame, click the **Set Out Point** button. This only affects the current scene. You can also add cuts while playback progresses.

3. Click the **Add Selection to Media Pane** button to add the retained scenes to your Media pane. The scenes will be named separately and will show in your Media pane.

If detecting scenes in a large video file, a progress bar appears until all scenes have been processed (click **Cancel** if you want to abort the process). You can still manage scenes while this is in progress.

Scene detection sensitivity

You can adjust the sensitivity of MoviePlus's scene detection simply by adjusting the **Threshold** slider in the Scenes dialog. An average scene detection value is set to detect scenes but you can adjust the detection sensitivity, resulting in a different number of scenes. Moving the slider to the left results in fewer scenes, moving to the right results in a greater number of detected scenes.

Trimming

With audio or video clips, both duration and playback speed come into play. Most often, you'll want to shorten a clip without altering its playback speed— this is usually called **trimming**. For example, media files seldom begin or end exactly where you'd like; there may be extra frames at the beginning or end, or you may want to use a short section from the middle of the file. The solution is to trim the media file—adjusting its start and end point, called "in" and "out" points, to include just the section of video you want.

Clips stored in your Media pane are usually trimmed in a Trim dialog **before** committing them to the storyboard (or timeline). The dialog shows the clip's frame preview and the clip's timeline (with ruler), from which trimming can be applied.

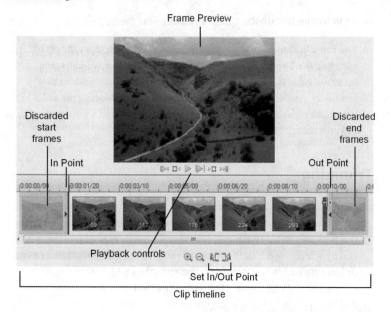

Frame Preview

Discarded
start
frames

Discarded
end
frames

In Point

Out Point

Playback controls

Set In/Out Point

Clip timeline

To trim a clip:

1. In the Media pane, either:

    ○ Select a clip and click ✎ **Trim**.
    OR

    ○ 🖉 Trim On the storyboard (or timeline), select a video clip and
    click the **Trim** button.

2. From the **Trim** dialog, for trimming visually by frame:

    ○ ▸⊏ ⊏◂ Hover your mouse cursor over the furthest left (or
    right) edge of the Clip's timeline so that it changes to the **Set In
    Point** (or **Set Out Point**) cursor, then drag the mouse to the right
    (or left) to trim away the start (or end) of your clip.

Or, to trim to a specific time/frame (using the Frame Preview):

1. Click on the ruler and drag the time indicator to the frame where you wish to trim before (or after), or use the controls under the frame preview for accurate frame-by-frame navigation.

2. Click the 🎞 **Set In Point** (or 🎞 **Set Out Point**) button. The unwanted portion of the clip will appear in grey shading.

3. To check the trimmed clip, click the ▷ **Play Trimmed** button.

4. Click the **OK** button.

🎞 The clip will show the adjusted Start or End time in the Media pane (click **Change View Style** for a Detailed view).

Previewing your project

The Video Preview pane will help you check that your movie editing is going according to plan... you can preview your project at any time; MoviePlus will begin playing your video, will compose a realistic end result from the contents of your all video tracks, and will incorporate all transitions, effects, and other envelopes on the fly. Audio levels can be checked at the same time.

You can even continue editing your project while the preview is playing as your edits will be incorporated into the preview in real-time.

The lower **playback controls** operate much like your DVD player controls and allow you to navigate around your project during preview.

Go to Start
Jumps to the start of your project.

Previous Frame
Jumps to the previous frame in your project.

Click the **Play** or **Pause** button to start and pause the video preview, respectively. On play, the preview will begin from the current preview marker's position.

Press the Space bar to play and pause.

Click the **Stop** button (or ESC key) to stop your video preview and reset the preview back to where it originally started.

Next Frame

Jumps to the next frame in your project.

 Go to End

Jumps to the end of your project.

 Shuttle

Allows you to vary the preview playback speed and direction by dragging from the centre point to the left (to reverse) or to the right (to fast forward); release the mouse to snap back to normal play speed. This is known as "trick play".

The buttons at the top of the pane offer preview options to optimize the pane's usage.

 The **Full Screen** button switches the Video Preview pane between normal and full screen display.

 For multi-monitor users, you can use this button to view your Video Preview pane on additional monitors. Simply enable the "Monitor *x*" option from the drop-down list (where *x* is the monitor number)—this also changes to full screen display (click the Full Screen button to revert).

 In Storyboard mode, the **Add Caption** button can be used to add one or more text objects onto the currently selected clip. Once added, the button is labelled **Add more text** for adding additional text. Timeline mode lets you add text via the latter button on a selected text clip (see Adding text on p. 169).

The **Pan** button lets you drag an area of your video around the pane. When used with the **Zoom in** button, this allows for more detailed analysis of screen areas.

The **Zoom In** and **Zoom Out** buttons let you focus in or out on the video as a whole.

The **AutoFit** button zooms the preview in or out so that it fits in the Video Preview pane.

The **TV Safe Borders** button switches on/off a translucent border (coloured in red, 10% of frame size, 50% opacity) placed over your video preview. This is used as a guide to help prevent titles and movie action from being cropped when your movie is played back on some older CRT TVs.

Use **TV Preview (via DV)** in **Tools>Options>Preview** to check your project while fine-tuning the size of the TV Safe border, in percentage increments, until the border just disappears during preview. Adjustments to border size (in percent), colour and opacity are made in **Tools>Options>Preview**.

The flyout allows the currently displayed frame to either be saved to an image file (use **Save Frame...**) or copied to the Clipboard (**Copy Frame**); the image can then be pasted as a graphic into a photo editing program, e.g. Serif PhotoPlus. Saving a frame adds the created image to your Media pane (Project tab).

Checking audio levels

The Levels meter provides a visual indication of current audio levels in your project. If levels peak above 0 dB (i.e. digital clipping occurs) to show red indicators, it's recommended to reduce **Gain** until clipping doesn't occur. See Volume and pan on p. 159.

Editing in
Storyboard mode

Storyboard basics

If needed, click the  button if you're in Timeline mode.

Storyboard mode provides the user with a simplified approach to movie making. If you're a beginner to video editing or you've no requirement for more complex multi-track editing techniques, the **storyboard** offers an easy-to-use workspace to build up your project and visualize different scenes in your movie. The easy-to-use storyboard is particularly suited to at creating quick-to-share photo slideshows.

Storyboarding itself has its origins in the animated cartoon industry, notably Walt Disney studios. By laying out cartoon cells in a time-based strip the cartoonist can add, rearrange, and remove individual cells to create a finished movie. The concept is exactly the same in MoviePlus—where a visual layout is created as it is to be seen by your audience. The difference being that cartoon cells are replaced by video clips, image clips, and text clips.

A major strength of the Storyboard mode is its simplicity. You'll only see options, buttons, and dialogs that are needed for simple projects with the more advanced multi-video-track editing controls being hidden in another mode, called the Timeline mode (see p. 69). Think of the Storyboard and Timeline modes as being like two sides of a coin—you can flip between modes to jump between basic and advanced use any time you like.

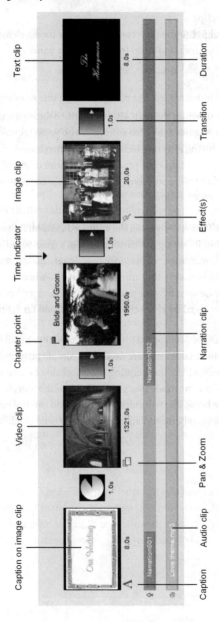

Text clip — Duration — 8.0s

Transition — 1.0s

Image clip — 20.0s — Effect(s)

Time Indicator

Chapter point — Bride and Groom — 1950.0s — Narration clip

Narration002

Video clip — 1321.0s — Pan & Zoom

Caption on image clip — 8.0s — Audio clip — Caption

Narration001

Love theme.mp3

Video and image clips

Video and image clip thumbnails, representing your media elements, appear on the storyboard by drag-and-drop from the Media pane.

Text clip

A text clip can be added for use as a static or rolling title or as credits. The clip has its own duration, and can be treated as for video/image clips. Additional text, as separate text objects, can be added onto the clip. See Adding text on p. 169 for more information.

Narration and audio clips

A narration clip is added under your video or image clips after recording from a microphone. Such purple-coloured clips reside on their own strip. Likewise, green-coloured audio clips show on a strip that lies below the narration strip. Use both in combination for commentary over background music (e.g., soundtracks).

Caption

Static or animated captions can be added to any clip. They are superimposed onto the clip and, like text clips, can adopt a preset text style or be customized. Caption text can appear for the clip's duration or for a shorter time.

Transition

A cross-fade transition of fixed duration is added between clips by default. The default transition can be swapped for another and have its duration altered. See Applying transitions on p. 55 for more information.

Chapter point

The ⚑ icon and supporting text label (e.g., Bride and Groom) indicate that a marker, used exclusively for DVD menus, is associated with the clip. Your DVD menu will include your chosen clip as a chapter, which can be clicked to play from that point in your movie. The chapter point is added from the equivalent button on the Storyboard toolbar. See Menu Designer: Editing Chapter Properties on p. 192 for more information.

Effects

The 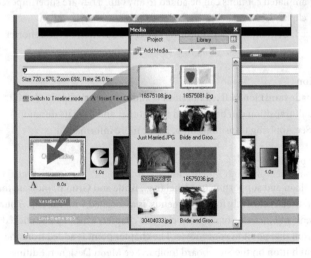 **Effects** icon indicates that an effect has been applied to the clip. Click the icon to view currently applied effects in the Properties pane (Effects tab). See Applying effects on p.135.

Duration

The duration is the time the clip or transition will be displayed on screen. Video clip durations cannot be edited, but for text clips, image clips and transitions, click under their thumbnails to edit their values.

Adding media files

Media files show in your Media pane after capture, download or import (see Adding media files to your project on p. 27). Once present, it's a great idea to arrange the order of the files prior to adding them to the storyboard (see p. 29). This avoids having to rearrange clips in bulk on your storyboard itself. Once you're happy with the order you can add the media to the storyboard.

To add media to the storyboard:

1.   From the Media pane, select your media, either:

  ○   Use marquee select (to lasso files under a selection region).
      OR
      Use **Shift** key and click (to select a range of adjacent files).
      OR
      Use **Ctrl** key and click (to select a range of non-adjacent files).
      OR
      press **Ctrl+A** (to select all files).

2.   Drag selected media onto your storyboard. If the storyboard is empty,
      drag your clips directly into the empty workspace. Video or image clips
      go to the "Drop clips here" target areas, while audio clips snap onto
      horizontal audio or narration strips below the thumbnails.

      If video clips are already present, insert your clip between
existing clips. An insertion point indicates where your clip is to be
placed.

Multiple clips will be added one by one along your storyboard.

Selecting clips

When you are editing your movie and have already added a range of media
clips to your storyboard, all your editing operations (including moves, trims,
properties changes and other adjustments) are carried out on the selected
clip. Clip selection is straightforward but several options can be used for
multiple selection.

To select a single clip:

○   Click on the clip.

To select multiple clips:

○   Use **Shift** key and click (to select a range of adjacent clips).
    OR

○   Use **Ctrl** key and click (to select a range of non-adjacent clips).
    OR

○   Press [⬜ Select all clips] on the Storyboard toolbar or **Ctrl+A** (to
    select all clips).

When selected, the clip's thumbnail
will be outlined to show that it is
selected.

Arranging clips

The storyboard is a workspace that arranges clips automatically as they are
dragged to the storyboard. As such there may not be a necessity to rearrange
clips if the clip order is as intended. Realistically, it's often the case that you
may want to further modify the clip order.

Once on the storyboard, an individual clip can be moved by drag and drop.
The vertical marker indicates the target location for the moved clip.

2345.0s   45545.0s   34342.0s

You can also copy and paste a clip by using options from the Edit menu.
Both methods can also be carried out on multiple clips simultaneously.

Deleting clips

- To remove a clip, select it and press the **Delete** key. By multiple
  selection, you can remove more than one clip at the same time. Use
  Ctrl-click to select non-adjacent clips, **Shift**-click for adjacent clips.

Resizing clips

If your added video or image clips are a different size and shape to your
project settings, MoviePlus will not resize your media to fit the project size,
leaving either "black" bars (letterboxing) showing in the available space.
Although you see black, the letterboxing is actually transparent (you're really
seeing the default project background showing through).

The shape of the video in the Video Preview pane is determined by your
project settings; if your clip properties and your project settings are different,
you can decide what to do about the variance, i.e. you can leave the media
with letterboxing or correct it via cropping.

Cropping removes unwanted borders either automatically by fitting to the
Video Preview pane or by defining a crop area you draw yourself (anything
outside the area is discarded); the clip is resized to fit the project. While used
frequently on image clips (of unusual dimensions or if in Portrait
orientation), you can also apply cropping to video clips—although it's
important to ensure items of interest are not cropped out throughout the
video clip's duration.

To resize a clip:

1. Select the clip.

2. Click [Fit] from the context toolbar and pick a resizing option from the drop-down list.

Letterbox - This is not normally set manually but can be used to override auto-cropping if this is deemed too excessive an action (if the clip's edges need to be preserved rather than removed by cropping).

Crop - This crops the clip to make it fit with the project size thus removing any letterboxing. The clip's aspect ratio is maintained so that the taller (or wider) areas are left outside the visible part of the project. See Cropping on p. 92 for more information.

Stretch - Stretches your clip horizontally or vertically to match the project video size—removing the letterboxing effect, but changing the clip's aspect ratio.

Custom - Launches a dialog that lets you remove everything outside a defined crop area. Size the crop area by moving corner or side handles then position the crop area again by dragging; The clip will resize to fit the crop area. The clip's aspect ratio is maintained by default. Drag a side handle to alter aspect ratio.

> You can double-click on the crop area to reset its size back to the project's dimensions.

> By default, clips that almost fit your project will crop (only if <3% difference between clip and project size) or letterbox (>3% difference). DVD clips in a VCD project will crop.

Applying transitions

MoviePlus supports many different transition types. For example, you can dissolve (**Cross-Fade**) between one clip and the other, or apply a variety of patterned wipes that use a moving edge or outline. Transitions such as **Iris Wipe**, **Cross-Blur** and **Zoom & Spin** are very popular in movie editing and are, of course, fully supported. MoviePlus can also produce some awe-inspiring 3D transitions—choose from 3D blinds, 3D Swap, 3D Flip, 3D Tumble, 3D Page Roll, to name but a few.

Transitions are displayed as inter-clip thumbnails in Storyboard mode, which change according to transition applied (the thumbnail represents the transition's function). The transition's duration is shown under its thumbnail. Some examples include:

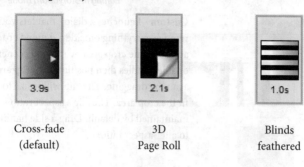

Cross-fade	3D	Blinds
(default)	Page Roll	feathered

Each transition is applied to the start of a clip—this is called an In transition.

To change a transition's duration:

- Click the duration time under the transition thumbnail, enter a new value, then press the **Enter** key.

Changing this value will automatically "ripple" all other subsequent clips along the storyboard with respect to time.

To replace a transition:

1. Select one or more transitions on the storyboard. For multiple transitions, **Ctrl**-click on each transition one-by-one; for all transitions click the **Select all transitions** button.

2. Click [Transition Gallery] on the context toolbar.

3. From the dialog, choose a category from the upper window. In the lower window, review the presets available (their names indicate their intended function). Select a preset, e.g. 3D Page Roll.

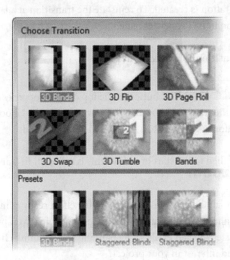

4. Click **OK**.

> ⊞ For a quick way to replace transitions, open the Galleries pane, select the **Transitions** button, then drag and drop a transition thumbnail onto your transition.

> Hover over any preset to see a preview of how your transition will look!

To modify a transition:

1. Select the transition thumbnail.

2. From the transition's Properties pane, alter the transition's' properties at the bottom of the pane.

To delete a transition:

○ Simply select a transition and press the **Delete** key.

The result is simply a cut: in less than the blink of an eye, the last frame of the first clip is replaced by the first frame of a second clip. In reality a cross-fade transition of zero duration is created. To reinstate the transition at a later date, give it a duration in its Properties pane.

To save a modified transition to a new name:

● Click the ⬚ Add to Gallery button at the top of the Properties pane. Once named, the transition appears as a new preset in the Choose Transition dialog.

Using pan and zoom

Pan and zoom effects can be used on any clip, but the effect really comes into its own when used on image clips. Rather than displaying clips that always display at the same size, you can easily apply panning and zooming effects that create variety and interest in your project.

The effect is applied by using a dual-pane dialog, the left-hand **Start** pane representing the start of the clip and the right-hand **End** pane, the end of the clip. Simply adjusting the resizable selection area in each pane sets the zoom level or pan position.

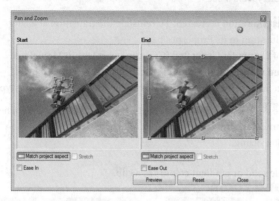

To pan and zoom your clip:

1. Click the clip on the storyboard (or timeline).

2. Select the [🗂 Pan & Zoom] button on the context toolbar.

3. From the dialog's **Start** pane, drag a corner or edge control handle (for maintaining aspect ratio or unconstrained sizing) on the selection area. Use the **Alt** key to resize the area in relation to the centre of the area (rather than the opposite corner or edge). Once sized, reposition the area with the hand cursor. Click the **Reset** button to reset each selection area back to the default size.

4. Adjust the area on the End pane in a similar way.

5. (Optional) Click **Match project aspect** on either pane to make the aspect ratio of that pane's selection area match that of your project.

6. (Optional) Check **Ease In** or **Ease Out** on respective panes to apply a non-linear rate of change to your pan and zoom (Quadratic slow).

7. Click **Close** to save your resized or repositioned areas.

The result is two sized areas which, on playback, MoviePlus will pan and zoom between according to the position and size of each area, respectively.

Using CG clips

Several types of Computer Generated (CG) clips exist within MoviePlus. They differ from video or audio clips in that they are not captured by camcorder, but are created from within MoviePlus itself. The following types of CG clip are available:

Backgrounds

To apply simple solid or gradient colours as a clip.

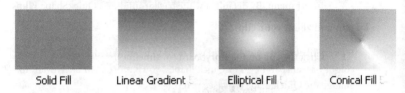

Solid Fill   Linear Gradient   Elliptical Fill   Conical Fill

QuickShapes

To add modifiable drawn shapes such as stars, hearts, spirals and many more.

Applying a background clip can be used to introduce colour either as part of a fade-in or fade-out, or as a background to text. Other uses include recolorizing semi-opaque video clips and masking shapes or text over a background colour.

For QuickShapes, a wide variety of commonly used shapes, including boxes, arrows, hearts, spirals and others are available. QuickShapes are really useful ready-made objects for introducing filled shapes, or for use in techniques such as masking.

What CG clips all share is that they are managed in a very similar way within MoviePlus, i.e. they can have colour, transparency and effects applied.

To apply a CG clip:

1. In Storyboard mode, select a clip (the clip before which the CG clip will be added).
   OR
   On the timeline, position your time indicator on the timeline.

2. Select your chosen CG clip type from the **CG Clip>** option on the Insert menu. By default, a white background or a QuickShape Ellipse is added to your timeline.

It's very likely that your CG clip will need to be modified, either to change its colour or transparency. For QuickShapes, you'll more than likely want to change the QuickShape type (see p. 65).

You'll find some ready-to-go sample gradient backgrounds or QuickShapes in the Media pane (Library tab), under Samples>Fills or Samples>Quickshapes. Simply drag to your storyboard or timeline.

Adjusting a clip's colour

MoviePlus offers a number of ways to apply colour to CG clips in MoviePlus. You can apply solid or gradient colours to any clip's fill.

A new colour is selected from a spectrum of preset colours or from a Colour Picker (both accessible via the **Edit Fill...** button on the clip's Properties pane).

For gradient fills you can adjust the gradient path of any gradient fill and the colours used to make up the gradient.

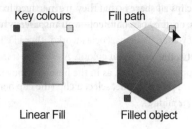

Key colours Fill path

Linear Fill   Filled object

Adjusting a clip's transparency

Transparency is great for highlights, shading and shadows, and simulating "rendered" realism. It can make a huge difference between your clips looking "flat" and appearing with depth and snap. MoviePlus fully supports variable transparency and lets you apply solid or gradient transparency to your CG clips.

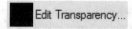

Edit Transparency...

Like fills, transparency can be applied from the clip's Properties pane. Select the **Edit Transparency...** button and choose a percentage **solid** transparency (via slider) or pick from a spectrum of preset **gradient** transparencies. If necessary, you can edit the transparency path.

- **Solid** transparency distributes the transparency evenly across the object.

- **Gradient** transparencies (Linear, Ellipse, and Conical), provide a simple gradient effect, with a range from clear to opaque.

Varying the transparency of a CG clip gives the effect of variable erasure, but it leaves the original object intact—you can always remove or alter the transparency later. Transparencies work rather like fills that use "disappearing ink" instead of colour. A gradient transparency varies from more "disappearing" to less, as in the hexagon above.

To save your CG clip:

○ Change the clip's name, then click the 🖫 Add to Media pane button at the top of the clip's Properties pane. The animation will appear in the Media pane's currently selected tab.

Fading with backgrounds

At the beginning or end of your project you can introduce a fade in or fade out by using a background clip. Such clips can be editable gradient fills (linear, ellipse and conical) as well as solid colours. They can equally be applied between clips to act as a coloured interlude (possibly with added captions).

○ On the storyboard, using a fade in as an example, you can introduce a background clip before the initial clip (**Insert>CG Clip>Background**).

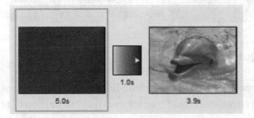

○ On the timeline, you can do the same but ensure the time indicator is set to the start of your project. If the clip you want to fade in to is already at the left edge of your timeline, leaving no room for the background clip at the beginning of the timeline, you should move your video/image clip(s) further down the timeline, creating some room at the start of your project. If you've already created a complex composition with multiple clips and tracks—so moving the first clip would disrupt the rest of your project—MoviePlus can move all of your later clips at the same time by using Rippling.

Other fading methods (timeline)

- For a colour fade, replace any transition with a Colour-Fade transition (either from the Properties pane's Galleries button or via drag/drop from the Galleries pane). Apply between clips, or at the start/end of your first or last clip.

- For a fade to/from black, you can fade clips in or out to black if they reside on your lowest video track. Simply drag the Cross-Fade transition's on your clip right or left (below) for a fade in or out, respectively.

More about QuickShapes

You're more than likely to swap the default Ellipse for a more applicable shape. An impressive selection of QuickShape types can be chosen from, and once you've picked a type, you can further morph its shape—all from within the QuickShape's Properties pane. The ability to further alter the appearance of any QuickShape type makes them more flexible and convenient than clipart pictures with similar designs.

To change your QuickShape type:

Once added to your timeline, the QuickShape type can be edited in its Properties pane (or by pressing **F4**). The lower portion of this pane hosts several options which will affect your QuickShape's appearance, i.e.

- Click the **QuickShape type** drop-down list to swap the default QuickShape Ellipse for your preferred design.

- The QuickShape preview window updates to show the current QuickShape, without colour fills or effect applied. This lets you focus on the main purpose of the window—to morph your QuickShape.

> The **Stretch to project size** checkbox, if checked, will ensure that the QuickShape will fully occupy the frame size.

To morph your QuickShape design:

- In the preview window, select a square control handle appearing next to the shape. Different QuickShapes have different handles. To find out what each handle does for a particular shape, move the control handles while reading the Status Bar. You can alter shapes dramatically with combinations of control handle adjustments. It's best to experiment!

For example:

- Dragging the handles on a Polygon will change the number of sides to make a triangle, pentagon, hexagon, or other polygon.

- Dragging the handle on a Rectangle alters the box corners to make them more or less rounded.

- Dragging the handles of a Star will alter its inner or outer radius, the number of points and the extent to which the points twist.

Editing in
Timeline mode

Timeline basics

Introduction

Click the 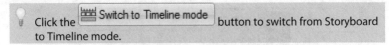 button to switch from Storyboard to Timeline mode.

For more advanced projects (compared to simpler storyboard-driven projects), the timeline lets you organize all your video and audio footage on **multiple tracks**, sequence clips one after the other, add and edit envelopes, effects, and so much more. The timeline offers the equivalent of all the manual editing operations that traditional movie editors need and it allows for post-production alterations.

The timeline has two basic dimensions, height and length. Horizontal length relates to the duration of your project: your timeline has markings along a ruler to indicate the passing of time, starting with zero at the left of the timeline. Any clips added to your timeline will follow a playback sequence from left to right. You can position the start point for previews (or the point at which you'd like to perform an edit) using a vertical marker called the **Time indicator**—this shows on both the timeline and as a preview marker in the Video Preview pane. The height of the timeline is related to the number of video or audio tracks used—you'll need to introduce more tracks if tackling advanced editing techniques including overlays, masking, blue-screening etc.

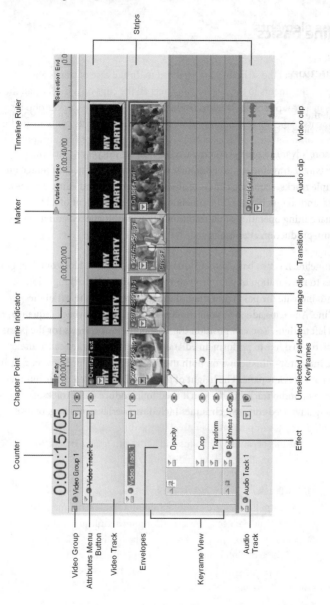

Strips

Timeline Ruler

Marker

Time Indicator

Chapter Point

Counter

Selection End

Video clip

Audio clip

Transition

Image clip

Unselected / selected Keyframes

Effect

Video Group

Attributes Menu Button

Video Track

Envelopes

Keyframe View

Audio Track

Timeline elements

Headers

Headers control the strip they are attached to. In the case of tracks and groups, adjustments to the header can affect all the clips on a track or all the tracks in a group (or both), respectively. You can select the track/group by clicking its name, mute (and unmute) to disable or enable its contents in the project composition, and display track/group envelopes for opacity and transform (video tracks/groups) or volume and pan (audio tracks/groups); a clip's crop envelope may also be shown along with its opacity and transform envelope. Track-wide effects may also be displayed.

The header may also show a clip's envelope or applied effects—these attributes are revealed by clicking its ⊡ **Attributes** button, and selecting an attribute.

Strips

Strips are the horizontal "stripes" running the length of the timeline (to the right of the headers section) that can store your clips. Each strip allows you to edit and arrange clips, as well as edit their effects, transitions, and envelopes. Each strip is accompanied by a header to its left.

Video/Image/Audio Clip

A clip is a media element; an "object" you can place on a timeline track. Clips can also include Computer-Generated (CG) clips (backgrounds, text, and QuickShapes). It's important to appreciate the difference between clips, tracks and groups because MoviePlus will allow you to add effects, for instance, to each or all of them with differing results.

Video/Audio Track

A track is just a straightforward combination of a single strip and its header. You can add multiple clips to a track by dropping a multiple selection from the Media pane onto your track's strip. The clips will be added to the timeline in succession with a default overlap. You can apply effects and envelopes (like opacity or a transform) to tracks, which will have a resulting effect on all the clips on that track. MoviePlus supports multiple audio and video tracks so that it is possible to compose more complicated projects with "layers" of video using fades to reveal underlying layers.

Additional Caption or Music tracks may show if you've created text or adopted some background music in Storyboard mode. A Narration track is created when you record narration (the narration clip is stored on this track).

Video/Audio Groups

MoviePlus supports audio and video groups (and effect groups). These are not only a way of keeping complex compositions tidy, you can also choose for effects—including the partial revealing of video using masks—to be applied to selected tracks only by placing them inside a group. The **View** menu also has an option to **Show Master Groups**, a top-level group to allow you to mute, apply effects to, or adjust envelopes for all video or all audio at once.

Keyframe View

When you add an envelope or effect to a clip, track, or group, or when you want to edit an existing envelope, effect or transition, the **Keyframe View** is displayed directly underneath the clip, track, or group.

Keyframes

Keyframes are points along a strip associated with a clip, track, or group's attributes (envelope, effect, or transition). The keyframe stores your chosen settings for use at a specific point of time along your timeline. Using more than one keyframe along a strip, MoviePlus automatically (and gradually) changes from one keyframe's settings to the next keyframe's settings as time passes between them. For example, on an opacity envelope, a keyframe at time zero with a setting of 0% opacity followed by another keyframe two seconds later with a setting of 100% would cause a gradual "fade in" effect over a period of two seconds. The keyframes can have their properties modified in the Properties pane when selected, and can be moved along the timeline to different points.

Envelopes, Effects and Transitions

Any time a clip, track, or group's Keyframe View is displayed via a common **Attributes menu**, the strips that show belong to one or more attributes of that object. Each attribute can be of type envelope, effect, or transition, and are grouped together for easy management. Normally you'll see envelopes, effects or transitions, but not all three attribute types all at once (this saves valuable timeline space). Each clip, track, or group cannot possess more than one envelope of the same type; only two transitions can be set on any single clip (you can't set a transition on a track). There is no restriction on the number of effects a clip, track, or group can have.

Marker
Markers act as guides on your timeline to indicate key time location or events that occur within your project. They can be labelled, positioned and navigated equally.

Chapter point
A chapter point is a type of marker that is used exclusively for disc creation. Each chapter point placed on your timeline defines the start of your chapters shown in your disc menu.

Set Selection Start/End
Selection markers set a start and end range on your timeline within which any encompassed clips will be either pre-rendered (for optimized preview performance) and/or exported to file, PSP, or iPod. The markers apply to all clips, tracks and groups down the entire height of the timeline. Limiting your export range is ideal for sharing only a chosen section of the movie, rather than the whole movie.

Time indicator
The time indicator, the blue vertical line you can see spanning the height of the timeline and its ruler, is most easily thought of as your editing marker. It allows you to set a precise position for splits and trims, allows clips and Keyframes to be accurately positioned on your project timeline, and can be used along the timeline ruler to play back a preview of your project from that point. You can also position your time indicator over the start/end of a clip then single-click to set a precise time indicator position. The time indicator is also shown in the Video Preview pane to indicate your playback position during playback.

Ruler

The ruler runs along the top of the timeline and shows you the current time range for the visible part of your project. You can zoom in or out of the timeline using a mouse wheel to display more or less of your project timeline on screen. A single-click on the ruler will position the time indicator marker for editing or video preview. You can alter your ruler units using the **View** menu's **Ruler Units** flyout. The default setting of "Time and Frames" is in the format *hh:mm:ss/ff*, representing hours, minutes, seconds and frames (of video), respectively.

Counter

The counter sits at the top-left of your timeline and shows you time at the time indicator. It uses the format set in the **View** menu's **Ruler Units** flyout.

Clip/track indicators and buttons

An LED in the top-left corner indicates if the clip (or track) is included in the composition (green) or if it is temporarily disabled (red). If you mute a track/group, the track/group header and each clip on that track/group would show a red LED to indicate that they are disabled. Clips also have blue triangular handles at each end that can be dragged to introduce an automatic cross fade (the fade can be replaced with a different transition by dragging and dropping a transition preset onto the clip's blue transition bar).

Attributes menu

On clips and track/group headers—clicking the **Attributes** button displays an **Attributes menu**, which is used to show envelopes, effects or transitions applied (along with their keyframes). The button will display in different colours according to selection and if the object's attributes have been modified, i.e.

Grey/White. Attributes unselected and unmodified.

Red/White. Attributes selected and unmodified.

Grey/Yellow. Attributes unselected and modified.

Red/Yellow. Attributes selected and modified.

Mute

Any clip, track or group can be muted at any time during video preview. You may want to temporarily switch off an audio track while you are editing and previewing the same track again and again. Equally, you may want to mute or "black out" a particular clip while testing your project.

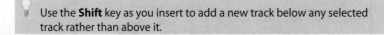 Muting is possible by switching on or off the respective **Mute** buttons on a video or audio track's header. For a video or audio clip, you can right-click and select the **Mute** option.

To keep the attribute(s) on permanent display, click the drawing pin in the header of your clip, track or group's attributes strip. Click again to hide.

Adding and arranging tracks

In Timeline mode, a single video and audio track are displayed on the timeline by default; these are named Video Track 1 and Audio Track 1. These empty tracks will allow a video and its linked audio clip (if present) to be dragged onto each track from the Media pane.

To add extra tracks:

- Choose **Video Track** or **Audio Track** from the **Insert** menu. The track is inserted above any existing tracks of the same type.

Use the **Shift** key as you insert to add a new track below any selected track rather than above it.

To change the track order:

- Drag the appropriate track header further up or down the stack of headers at the left of the timeline. You'll see a grey line between tracks and a place cursor where your track can be inserted. Release the mouse button to place.

The above example reorders two simple video tracks (selected Video Track 3 is dragged to be placed above Video Track 2).

Adding media files

Media files show in your Media pane after capture, download or import (see Adding media files to your project on p. 27). Once present, it's a great idea to arrange the order of the files prior to adding them to the timeline (see p. 29). This avoids having to rearrange clips in bulk on your timeline itself. Once you're happy with the order you can add the media to the timeline.

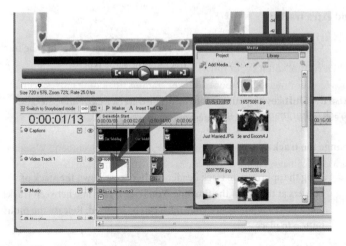

To add media to the timeline:

1. From the Media pane, select your media, either:

   ○ Use marquee select (to lasso files under a selection region).
   OR
   Use **Shift** key and click (to select a range of adjacent files).
   OR
   Use **Ctrl** key and click (to select a range of non-adjacent files).
   OR
   press **Ctrl+A** (to select all files).

2. Drag selected media onto your timeline. Multiple clips will be added one by one along your timeline. Tracks suitable to specific clip types will be offered.

Where you drag your clips onto the timeline is up to you, the area is "freeform"; video and image clips must be located on video tracks, and of course audio on audio tracks. It is normal to place clips in an empty spot and move them to the desired precise spot if necessary afterwards. Being placed on a track higher up the timeline will mean your clip could obscure underlying elements; underlying tracks are perfect as backgrounds behind video, image, or text overlays.

Selecting clips

When you are editing your movie and have already added a range of media clips to your timeline, all your editing operations (including moves, trims, properties changes and other adjustments) are carried out on the selected object(s). So, let's cover how you go about selecting clips!

The good news is that you can simply click on clips to select them. Whether it's a video, image, audio, or text clip, a click will outline it in dark-blue to show you that it is selected. Track or group names (in the header) are highlighted in red.

Selecting multiple clips

You can select multiple clips (including clips that are linked) on your
timeline by three main methods:

- To select **non-adjacent** clips, hold the **Ctrl** key down on your
  keyboard and click each clip you would like to include in the selection.
  Ctrl+click again to remove a clip from the current selection.

- To select **adjacent** clips on a single track, click a clip at one end of your
  proposed selection range, hold the **Shift** key down and click on the
  clip at the other end. All clips in between, plus the selected clips, are
  selected.

- For **marquee selection**, hold your primary mouse button down and
  drag a rectangle on your timeline—anything touching (and also
  anything inside) the rectangle will become selected.

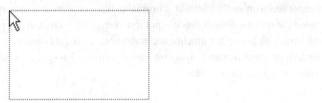

When multiple clips are selected, you can perform stretching on all clips
simultaneously.

To make your multiple selection a permanent feature of your timeline for
continuous easy editing, you can create a **Link** as described in Arranging
clips (see p. 82).

How selected objects are displayed

Object	Selection status
	Clip has been clicked and is selected (a dark-blue border appears around the object). You can now modify its properties in the Properties pane, and perform other operations (trim, fit, etc). Selecting a transition (e.g., Cross-Fade) also shows in dark blue.
	This audio clip is part of a Link (with the above video clip)—a pale-blue border is shown. When any object in the Link is selected, all other items in the Link take on this "pale-blue" selection highlight. Although not actually selected, edits will affect it.
	This clip has had one of its envelopes, effects, or transitions modified (e.g., a keyframe below the tracks in the Keyframe View area) as the Attributes button (circled) has changed from grey/white to red/yellow.

(Grey) A keyframe on an envelope, effect, transition, background, QuickShape or text strip. This keyframe is not selected.

(Red) A keyframe selected by single-click. You can now modify this keyframe's properties via the attributes Properties pane.

A track is selected when its name is highlighted. Other strip headers (clip strip headers, effects/envelope/transition strip headers) have a similar appearance.

This track has had one of its envelopes, effects or transitions modified.

Zooming, scrolling, seeking, and scrubbing

To see more or less of your project at one time or to navigate your project, you can perform various operations along your timeline.

Zooming

The Status Bar hosts a series of very useful tools for zooming your timeline.

 To see more detail on your timeline to make it easier to perform fine edits, click the **Zoom In** button or scroll your mouse wheel upwards. To see more of your project in the timeline area, click the **Zoom Out** button or scroll your mouse wheel downwards.

To see your entire project within the available timeline area—simply click the **Zoom to All** button.

If your time indicator is out of view due to a zoom operation or playback of your project preview, select **Scroll to Time Indicator** from the View menu to jump to the time indicator's current position.

Scrolling

To scroll the timeline horizontally, hold down the **Shift** key while using your mouse wheel, or to scroll vertically, hold down the **Ctrl** key.

It's also possible to drag your time indicator to the left or right edge of your window to scroll previously hidden parts of your timeline into view.

Seeking

The Video Preview pane also helps with some seek operations.

- The [icon] **Go to Start** and [icon] **Go to End** buttons let you jump to the beginning or end of your project, respectively.

- [icons] For fine tuning the position of the time indicator (i.e., frame stepping or frame advance), for instance to perform a trim operation at a specific frame of video, you can use the **Previous Frame** and **Next Frame** buttons.

- The [icon] **Shuttle** control allows you to vary the preview playback speed and direction by dragging from the centre point to the left (to reverse) or to the right (to fast forward).

Scrubbing

Scrubbing might seem an unusual term but it is an extremely useful feature! You may already know that clicking along the Ruler above the timeline sets your time indicator's position. However, if you click and drag along the ruler, MoviePlus will preview your project at the speed of the drag—as your mouse passes along the timeline in either direction, the preview will show you the current frame. This allows you to pass your mouse over an area of the timeline to preview a specific section without starting and stopping preview playback.

Arranging clips

Arranging clips on your timeline is crucial to building interesting, more complex projects—typically to create a rich multi-track multimedia project with the most popular video editing techniques. While the Storyboard mode offers a simple sequential clip-by-clip ordering, the Timeline mode offers more versatility and power to arrange clips where you want them.

Simple arrangement—clips following one another

When you want one clip—a video or image—to directly follow on from another clip, they need to touch each other on the timeline with no space in between them. When one "scene" follows another in this way, it's often referred to as a "cut" although you don't need to get the scissors out to achieve it with MoviePlus.

Simply drag clips along on the same track so that they are positioned next to each other. When two clips are close together the one you are dragging will snap into place. Multiple clips can be dragged onto the timeline with a default cross-fade transition overlap.

Making one clip appear on top of another

MoviePlus uses multiple tracks in a similar fashion to the way photo-editors (such as Serif's own PhotoPlus) use multiple layers. The question of whether you need to use multiple layers—or tracks in the case of MoviePlus—can be answered in the same way for both types of program... many compositions are perfectly fine with one "layer" but you can introduce some interesting effects by layering your images or videos on top of each other.

MoviePlus composes your video based on timeline content, working from the top downwards. If you have multiple tracks in your project with a full-size video on the top layer, it could well obscure all underlying tracks because you can't see through it... but if your top-most track (or clips on it) contains Images (with transparency), Background, QuickShape or Text clips with reduced opacity, resized video or images using a transform envelope, video with a mask applied or a Chroma Key effect, you will be able to see through to underlying tracks.

So, to make one clip an overlay appearing on top of other clips, add an additional video track (choose **Video Track** on the **Insert** menu), then place the video or image you would like to appear as an overlay on the top track. All tracks support images or video with transparency, and all tracks follow the same timeline, so objects are almost as easy to arrange when using multiple tracks as they are for single-track projects.

Deleting clips

Any selected clip on your timeline can be deleted by pressing the **Delete** key. Any accompanying linked clip will also be deleted, i.e. a video clip and its associated audio clip are removed simultaneously.

Linking clips together for easy editing

Automatically-linked clips

When you add a video clip to your timeline, you will normally find that two clips are added to your timeline—one video clip and one audio clip, on a video and audio track, respectively. This is because the video file contained both an audio and video stream that MoviePlus has separated for you for editing purposes. Because these two streams came from the same location, MoviePlus automatically links them together. When clips are linked, edits to one of the objects will affect other linked objects. If you select your video clip and perform a split, for instance, the linked audio clip will split in the same place.

When you select a clip it is highlighted in dark blue; any clips linked to it will adopt a "light blue" selection outline at the same time.

When moving clips, any linked clips on different tracks will move to new relative locations on the timeline providing there is enough space on each track for your clips to relocate to.

Manually-linked clips

You can manually create, edit, and destroy links of your own, too, to make a collection of clips easier to move or otherwise edit. The operations described below are provided in a right-click menu (**Link** option), but are also available from the **Edit** menu.

- **Create Link**: Establishes a link between two or more selected clips.

- **Add to Link**: If you've got linked files already selected, use **Ctrl**-click to select another clip to be linked, then select this option.

- **Remove from Link**: Select a file already linked, then choose this option to remove just the selected file from the link.

- **Destroy Link**: Click any linked file then select this option to unlink itself and all other files that are linked.

Temporarily disabling Linking

There are occasions where you may find the need to temporarily disable Linking, for instance when trying to trim clips that are part of a Link, where other linked clips start or end outside the range of the clip you are editing... in such instances some editing functions are unavailable because they cannot be applied to the entire contents of the Link group. Other reasons for unlinking include deleting an unwanted audio track and copying a clip independently of its linked clips. In such instances you would need to disable the **Linking** button on the timeline's context toolbar, perform your edit, then switch Linking back on using the same button.

Aligning frames

The **Align To Frames** option on the **Arrange** menu will enable and disable snapping to the nearest frame of video. Video frames are typically about 30 or 40 milliseconds apart (there's typically 25 or 30 frames per second of video), so you can choose whether your time indicator-based editing snaps to these divisions or is totally freeform. Frame snapping, or align to frames, is the normal mode to work with unless you are trimming audio to a very fine degree.

Rippling

Rippling is a design aid that takes some of the headache out of making room on your timeline, or taking up slack (empty) space on the timeline by keeping your clips' relative positions constant when you make edits (this also includes a clip's keyframes). Rippling saves you the effort of moving multiple clips for the sake of what is often a minor edit, perhaps to make room at the start of your project for titles or a new intro or the deletion of a section of video from the middle of a project. You can enable and disable Rippling using either the **Rippling** button on the timeline's context toolbar, or by using the command on the **Arrange** menu.

Moving clips

Rippling affects other clips (and their envelope, effect or transition's keyframes) starting at the same time or after the clip you are moving. When you move a clip, those other clips that start at the same point or later on the timeline will shuffle left or right to account for your move.

When trimming or extending the end of a clip

Rippling only affects other clips that both start after your edited clip starts and end after the end of your edited clip.

When trimming the start of a clip

Rippling affects other clips that start and end after the start of your edited clip, and it also moves your edited clip to the same "start time" it had before you trimmed its start, shuffling other affected clips at the same time.

Ripple mode

Rippling can be set to work in one of four modes: it can affect the track you are working on, all tracks of the same level (e.g., those within a group), all tracks on the same level including marker rippling, or the whole timeline (with marker rippling). The last two options allow markers to maintain their positions relative to the moved clips—otherwise marker positions will not alter when rippling takes place.

Rippling with complex projects

For complex multi-track projects, you might worry that Rippling won't manage all the necessary moves—don't worry, Rippling works regardless of the number and type of clips or tracks involved. Providing you have selected the appropriate **Ripple mode** as mentioned above, you can move a large number of clips that span multiple tracks by having Rippling enabled. Be sure to select an appropriate timeline zoom level when selecting and moving your clips—you may wish to use a low zoom level (to see all of your project) to make the move easy, but you might find that using a higher zoom level (seeing just a few small clips) allows you to more easily select and drag the correct clip. MoviePlus will automatically scroll the timeline in the direction of your drag until you centre your mouse to choose a "drop zone", but you could instead type a new start time for your selected clip in the Properties pane—Rippling works however a clip is moved.

Snapping

Snapping is a design aid that helps you achieve neat layouts. When you are moving objects around on the timeline (or trimming/stretching them), snapping makes your edit jump to the nearest clip, to the position of the time indicator, to the beginning of the timeline, and to a default transition overlap value.

By default, snapping is enabled, although you can switch it off from the **Arrange** menu. To control which elements do and do not get snapped to, or to adjust snap sensitivity, visit the **Snapping** tab (**Tools>Options**). Hold down **Alt** during your editing operations to temporarily switch snapping off (or on, if disabled).

Using groups

Groups serve a couple of important functions on MoviePlus's timeline. Firstly, they can help keep related tracks together for easy management. For instance, applying an effect to a video group means that all tracks within the group inherit the effect. For example, for a Solarize effect:

Video Group 1 contains Video Track 1 and Video Track 2 (but not the Background Video track). The Solarize effect has been applied to the Group (and therefore Tracks 1 and 2 simultaneously). Background Video is not subject to the Solarize effect.

The next main function for groups is more complicated but very useful, i.e. limiting the range of a transparency effect or mask. Masks and the Chroma Key effect are both methods of achieving transparency (see p. 119 and p. 123).

To add a video or audio group:

1. Select the video or audio track above which you want to insert a group.

2. Choose **Video Group** or **Audio Group** from the **Insert** menu.

Once you've created a group you have to then associate chosen tracks to the group.

To add a track to a group:

○ Drag and drop the track over the group header, i.e.

The track will be nested under the group if the operation is successful.

To drag a track out of a group, aim to drop the track at the bottom edge of the group or any header position that is as wide as the group's header.

If using video or audio groups, click the **Collapse/Expand** button to collapse the group's tracks, envelopes, or effects.

Applying opacity to groups

You can adjust the opacity of a group in two ways—either by adjusting the group's **Opacity** slider in the group's Properties pane, or by adjusting a group's opacity on its opacity envelope. For the latter method, click the ▼ **Attributes** button in the group header to reveal the **Attributes** menu—select Opacity to reveal an editable inline opacity envelope. This will allow you to fade the result of an affected section of video organized within a group, for instance, or to make a series of still image overlays appear translucent—without having to edit each clip or track in an identical way.

See Using envelopes on p. 94 for more information about revealing and editing envelopes in general.

Transforms—perspective, scaling, and motion

You can apply transforms, such as perspective effects, resizing, or animated motion, to video groups. Such an effect would allow for the composite result of a group to be used as an inset video, for instance. To learn how to edit a transform envelope, see Adjusting keyframes on p. 98.

Audio groups

It is possible to add audio tracks to audio groups to adjust overall volume and/or pan. Volume and pan envelopes allow for simple adjustments as well as introducing changing levels over time; please see Using envelopes and Adjusting keyframes on p. 94 and p. 98 for more information.

Master groups

Show Master Groups in the **View** menu lets you affect all the audio or video groups/tracks separately but all at once, by showing master groups on your timeline header region. There are two master groups, one for video and one for audio. The master groups each encapsulate all the video and audio of your project so you can adjust the master volume, for instance, by adjusting the volume envelope for the master audio group, or apply a final video effect to the entirety of the video in your project by applying it to the master video group.

If there's no need to use this, you should leave the option unchecked in the **View** menu.

Video effect groups

Video Effect groups are not used frequently but are essential if you wish to blend affected and unaffected video. The affected video would have cumulative effects applied, which could be blended in and out of the mix by adjusting the keyframes of the Video Effect Group's envelope.

Splitting clips

Timeline mode exclusively offers a very useful video editing tool for splitting any video clip into two at the currently set time indicator's position. Compare this to scene detection, carried out in the Media pane, which splits scenes automatically but offers an equivalent manual splitting option if needed. Generally speaking, you'll want to split clips in the Media pane in most instances.

Splitting a clip into two lets you insert another "filler" clip in between each split clip. You can perform multiple splits to create distinct sections of your clips for deletion.

To split a clip:

1.   Select the clip you would like to split.

2.   Position the time indicator on the ruler at the point you would like to make the split.

3.   Click the 🎬 **Split** button.

Cropping

You can perform simple crops on any clip by using the ⬜ Fit ▾ button in either Storyboard or Timeline mode (See Resizing clips on p. 53). This affects the clip for its entire duration. However, the power of the Timeline mode lets you change a clip's cropping over time (just as for transforming a clip).

The method for cropping and transforming over time is similar in the way it is applied, i.e. like a transform, cropping uses a dedicated envelope, which is accessible for any clip from the clip's Attributes menu. This **crop envelope** is displayed, controlled and modified as for any other envelope. It can host one or more keyframes along the envelopes length (called the strip) to dictate the crop selection area, i.e. each keyframe sets the crop area size at that time.

For a quick recap on envelopes and keyframes, see Using envelopes and Adjusting keyframes on p. 94 and p. 98.

MoviePlus opens up some interesting possibilities when cropping over time as you can pan in any direction, zoom, pan/zoom together and create panoramas. To make life easier, you can perform the above operations by adopting a pre-built crop envelope preset.

To use a crop envelope preset:

1.   Right-click a clip and choose **Apply Envelope...**.

2.   From the dialog, pick the crop folder, a crop preset from any child folder, then click on a preset under that folder.

3.   Click **OK**.

You'll notice the crop envelope appear under your clip.

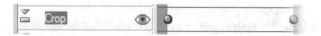

The envelope typically shows two keyframes, each storing the crop area's size at that time. The properties of the selected keyframe (⬤) show the sized crop area, e.g.

You can modify the envelope by adjusting the crop area on each keyframe in the envelope, and optionally saving the preset to a new name.

Alternatively, you can set the crop area manually by entering Top, Bottom, Left or Right percentage values (click the **Manual** drop-down option).

To save your modified envelope:

- Click the 🖫 Add to Gallery button in the envelope's Properties pane. You'll be asked for an envelope name. The envelope is saved to the root Crop folder of the Envelope dialog.

Cropping with masks

As a very powerful way of cropping irregular shaped objects (as opposed to cropping to square or rectangle areas), cropping video with masks involves using a simple image overlay to describe which areas of your video should remain visible and which areas should become transparent.

Masks are usually simple images made with a transparent region and a white region; when applied correctly in the MoviePlus timeline, these images affect underlying video, with white in the mask translating to visible regions of your video and transparency in your mask translating to transparent (cut/cropped) regions of the video. You can use this functionality to hide (or crop away) portions of your video that you do not want included. Masks allow for irregular cropping, cropping with soft edges, animated cropping; the possibilities are infinite, as are the number of mask images or videos you can create.

For more information, see Masking on p. 119.

Using envelopes

Envelopes in this context are not an item of stationery, they are a method of applying change to a clip, track or group's properties over time. Imagine an envelope as a hidden "track" that runs along with each clip, track, and group in your project and at specific times you determine how it changes its properties. Between the specific times you specify envelope settings, MoviePlus can calculate smooth changes to the properties.

There are different types of envelopes that all work in very similar ways for controlling cropping, opacity, and transforms for video clips, and volume and stereo pan for audio clips. Once you learn how to display and modify one type of envelope, you can apply the same principle to all other envelope types. However there is a distinction between some envelope types.

- **Opacity**, **Volume** and **Pan**: These simple envelopes can adjust the properties of an object over its duration on the timeline. They appear as thick strips because the envelope only affects one attribute (e.g., volume level). This lets you position buttons (called keyframes) in the vertical axis to create fade-ins or fade-outs of opacity, volume and pan. For example, a volume envelope could be used on an audio track to fade-in the sound at the start of your video.

- **Crop** and **Transform**: These more complex envelopes can also adjust the properties of an object over the timeline, but as they possess multiple properties which are often inter-related, they can't be easily represented on the timeline. Therefore, they appear as a thin strip stretching the duration of the clip, track or group, leaving the envelope's Properties pane to take on the configuration role. Here's a simple crop envelope, containing three keyframes.

Envelopes can be edited, copied, pasted and muted (to temporarily switch off its effect). Editing of the envelope is possible on the whole envelope or on individual keyframes within the envelope itself.

Displaying envelopes

Envelopes can be displayed as strips that show under the selected clip, track or group. Choose from the options below:

For clips

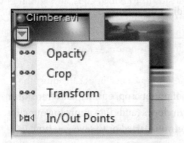

Click on the button on top of your clip to reveal an **Attributes** menu. When an opacity, crop or transform envelope is selected from the menu, the clip's **Keyframe View** is displayed directly below the clip.

All envelopes are shown in separate strips with your chosen envelope already selected. To change to a different envelope either click another envelope's name in the video header or click anywhere in the envelope strip on the timeline.

The button, being grey/white, will change colour to red/white when selected. If your envelope has been modified it will adopt a red/yellow colour.

For video tracks and groups

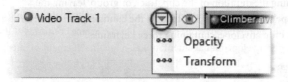

Click on the ▼ button in the header section of a selected track or group to reveal an **Attributes** menu. Like clips, selected envelopes and keyframes show under track or group.

Adjustments to envelopes will affect all clips on the track, or all tracks in the group. For example, adjustments to a video group's opacity envelope will result in opacity changes to the composite result of the group's contents. For example, if a video group contains four tracks each with a transform envelope that makes each track fill just one quarter of the visible area, all four videos would simultaneously have their opacity adjusted when you modify their group's opacity envelope. Groups are also used when cropping or masking video, so you may want to adjust the group's opacity—rather than individual tracks or clips.

Preset envelopes

MoviePlus provides a great selection of preset crop, opacity, and transform (video/image) and volume and pan envelopes (audio) to apply to your clips, tracks or groups. Use the presets to get you started or to save you time.

To apply an envelope preset:

1. Select the clip, track or group.

2. From the Attributes menu, select Opacity, Crop (clip only), or Transform to show its envelope.

3. From the Properties pane, select ⊞ Gallery... and from the dialog, navigate the tree menu structure and choose a preset envelope. Your envelope shows automatically under the object.

Editing envelopes

All envelopes are powerful because of the potential to manipulate existing or added keyframes along the envelope's length. This keyframe control is at the heart of not only envelope management, but also the management of effects and transitions, and is described in detail in Adjusting keyframes (see p. 98).

All envelopes have one default keyframe positioned at the start of the object, which defines how the envelope will operate either until the next keyframe on the timeline or for the duration of the clip, track or group.

Resetting envelopes

An envelope cannot be deleted but instead its resident keyframes can be deleted, effectively resetting the envelope back to its default state. Simply select the envelope and press the **Delete** key.

Copying and scaling envelopes

An envelope can be copied by right-clicking on its header and choosing **Copy**. When an envelope is copied to the clipboard, it can be pasted to another selected object to replace the existing envelope of that object, e.g. an opacity envelope from one clip will overwrite the opacity envelope of another video clip by copy and paste.

If an envelope is copied and pasted from one clip to another clip further down the timeline, associated keyframes can be optionally scaled so they are in proportion with the new clip. This is also useful if you are changing the total length of the track as the key frames are scaled to that new length. To do this, change each keyframe's **Keyframe Mode** to Proportional in the envelope's Properties pane. Another advantage of scaling is that you can save your own custom envelope to a new preset, safe in the knowledge that the keyframes are never stored with absolute times, and instead can be scaled easily to any object on the timeline in the future!

Saving envelopes

Add to Gallery To save your envelope to a new name (in the Properties
pane) along with your existing presets, use the **Add to Gallery** button in the
envelope's Properties pane. After providing a name, your new envelope is
saved in the envelope type's root folder.

Adjusting keyframes

The Keyframe View

When you add an envelope, effect or transition to a clip, track, or group, the
Keyframe View is displayed directly underneath the object as a white area,
e.g. for a clip.

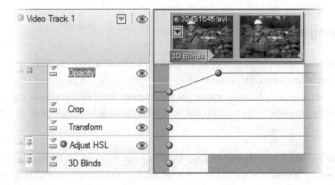

When you want to edit an existing envelope, effect or transition, click on
the grey/white button on your object to reveal a drop-down **Attributes**
menu. On selecting a menu item, the object's currently applied envelopes,
effects and/or transitions are shown in one or more strips directly under the
object (the button changes to red/white). Each strip allows you to induce
change over time, whether it's for an envelope, effect or transition. The points
in time that you specify such change are represented on these strips by
Keyframes (grey or red when selected).

The Attributes button will change to red/yellow if an envelope, effect or transition has been edited and then to grey/yellow when a modified object has all its strips hidden.

Once the Keyframe View is enabled, you will be able to edit envelopes and their keyframes, causing change over time.

What are keyframes?

A keyframe is the small grey circle that appears on the envelope, effect or transition strips. For tracks and groups there is a default keyframe at the start of the timeline. For selected clips, the default keyframe is set at the start of the clip, so when you move your clip its envelope also moves in synchronization.

Keyframes store information about the property you are editing. If we use opacity as an example, as it's such a simple property, MoviePlus is able to draw a line of a set height along the length of its opacity envelope to describe whether the current opacity value is high, low, or any stage in between (as shown).

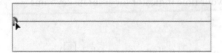

The initial single keyframe defines the opacity level by its vertical position in the envelope (see how the Properties pane's Opacity value changes as you drag the keyframe up and down).

You can modify keyframe properties when a keyframe is selected—click a grey (deselected) keyframe and it will turn red (selected).

Modifying the default keyframe

To modify the default keyframe you can either move it up and down within the strip (for some simple envelopes) or just click the keyframe to select it (it will turn red) then adjust its properties in the Properties pane (for complex envelopes, effects, or transitions). You can also move the keyframe further along the timeline to the right.

An important point about the first and last keyframes when moved is that their properties will extend to the beginning and end of the clip, track, or group.

Adding and modifying keyframes

To cause change over time (by changing an object's properties), it is essential to add and subsequently edit keyframes along the attribute's strip (for crops, transforms, effects, and transitions). For effects and transitions you'll need to apply them in advance.

Any added keyframe adopts the properties of the keyframe immediately preceding it on the timeline.

To add a keyframe:

1. (Optional) Position your time indicator for accurate keyframe placement.

2. Select the attribute from the Attributes menu (click ▼).

3. In the strip's header, select the attribute to add a keyframe to.

4. Hover the cursor along the object's strip until it changes to the Add cursor (+), then click to add the keyframe. If you've positioned your time indicator, hover over the point where the indicator intersects with the strip—you'll add a keyframe that snaps to an exact time.

You can also use the ⁺◉ Add Keyframe button on the Properties pane; this adds a keyframe at the current time indicator's position.

Whichever way keyframes are added, they can be arranged along a strip at chosen intervals (a keyframe is red when selected), i.e.

For some simpler envelopes such as opacity, pan and volume, you can add and edit keyframes as above but you can also drag the keyframe up or down to adjust the keyframe's properties directly. These envelope strips are designed to have more depth for this reason—great for fade-in and fade-outs on opacity and volume envelopes.

In this example, a volume envelope on an Audio track fades in at the start of a movie. MoviePlus draws the rate of volume change as a line between the keyframes.

Any keyframe can be modified via the Properties pane—simply select the keyframe (making it red) and then press **F4**. The Properties pane is shown for the keyframe.

Selecting keyframes

At some point you may want to select more than one keyframe at the same time—typically to cut, copy, or move keyframes. You can also change Interpolation or Keyframe Mode by right-clicking on multiple keyframes and accessing a flyout menu. MoviePlus lets you select multiple keyframes as for any other object on the timeline.

- Use **Ctrl**-click to select each keyframe in turn.
  OR

- Drag a marquee around a region containing your keyframes.

Moving keyframes

You can move one or more keyframes left and right along the strip which has the effect of moving them earlier or later along the timeline. For more precision, you can also set a selected **Keyframe time** position in the Properties pane.

Navigating keyframes

- Use the **Ctrl+<** and **Ctrl+>** keyboard shortcuts to **Select Previous Keyframe** and **Select Next Keyframe** on a strip (also available on the Edit menu).
  OR

- Use the button in the Properties pane.

Copying keyframes

Any selected keyframe can be copied to the clipboard. Simply select a single keyframe (or multiple keyframes with the **Ctrl** key), right-click and select **Copy**.

When keyframes are on the clipboard, they can be pasted into any attribute strip of the same type they came from. They will be pasted at the time indicator location.

If an envelope, effect or transition is copied and pasted from one clip to another clip further down the timeline, associated keyframes can be optionally scaled so they are in proportion with the new clip. This is also useful if you are changing the total length of the track as the keyframes are scaled to that new length.

To do this, change each keyframe's **Keyframe Mode** to Proportional in the envelope's, effect's or transition's Properties pane. Another advantage of scaling is that you can save your own custom envelope, effect or transition to a new preset, safe in the knowledge that the Keyframes are never stored with absolute times, and instead can be scaled easily to any object on the timeline in the future!

Altering rate of change between keyframes

By default, where you have two keyframes with different values, MoviePlus will gradually step from one range of settings to the next in a smooth manner—this is known as Linear interpolation. MoviePlus is interpolating (calculating) values between the keyframes and the change is linear, i.e. half way between the values you will have encountered half the required amount of change.

However, it's handy to be able to alter the rate of change, as in video production it's usually a good idea to aim for smoothness—sudden starts or ends to movement (as with other effects) is not always desirable and can sometimes detract from the video content.

To alter the rate of change between keyframes:

1. Right-click a keyframe, to view the **Interpolation** flyout. This offers handy previews of the rates of change as curved or straight lines, like a graph or chart.
   OR

   Select a keyframe, and in the keyframe's Properties pane, click the **More** option to reveal keyframe properties.

2. Choose an interpolation method via the **Interpolation** option.

Using the volume envelope example below, a right-click on the first keyframe will allow you to adjust the rate of volume change towards the second keyframe—a curve appears between keyframes.

The first keyframe is subject to a Quadratic Slow curve to start and end the fade-in slowly.

On occasion, you may wish to apply a Hold interpolation on a keyframe where, instead of change over time, the keyframe's properties remain constant for its duration. These are particularly useful on an audio clip's volume envelope where you may want to switch the volume on and off at specific points along the timeline (instead of fading).

Positioning keyframes

When you modify an object or you intend to copy and paste an attribute's strip to another object's attribute strip (of different length) you can choose various mode options to decide how MoviePlus will reposition a keyframe once it is copied.

- For an envelope, effect, or transition, the **Keyframe Mode** setting offers various positioning options for keyframes; this affects only the **currently selected** keyframe(s).

The setting, found in the **More** section of the attribute's Properties pane, can be one of the following:

- **Absolute**: keyframe does not move (default). Great for corresponding your keyframes to an event on the timeline.

- **Proportional**: keyframe moves in proportion to the new object's length (i.e., duration). Useful for creating presets (e.g., envelopes) whose keyframes will scale to any target object.

- **Relative to Start**: keyframe moves relative to the start of the object if its length is changed. Use for fade-ins.

Relative to End: keyframe moves relative to the end of the object if its
length is changed. Use for fade-outs.

If you want to apply the same Keyframe Mode to multiple keyframes, you
can select your keyframes, right-click, and pick a new setting from the flyout
menu.

> When keyframes have a **Keyframe mode** of "Absolute" they are affected
> by Rippling (if turned on). Other modes will be unaffected by rippling.

Applying transitions

Any time one piece of video ends and another begins, a transition takes place.
In its simplest form, the transition is simply a cut: in less than the blink of an
eye, the last frame of a clip is replaced by the first frame of a second clip.

In MoviePlus, the term "transition" applies to a more gradual way of
switching from one clip to another. If you add multiple media files from the
Media pane or overlap two clips slightly on the same or separate tracks, you
get a time-based change between them, shown as a blue region (as indicated
below). An In transition called "Cross-Fade" is added by default to the second
clip.

This rectangular-shaped region indicates that the transition is **automatic**.

> The default Cross-Fade transition type has no associated properties.
> However, all other transition types have associated properties, which can
> be modified at any time.

Another type of transition is a **manual** transition, which can be either an In
transition or Out transition. They are created manually at the start or end of
a single clip, respectively. The former can be useful as a fade-in on the first

clip at the start of a track (first example below). Conversely, an Out transition can be applied to the last clip in any track as a fade-out (second example below).

In Transition   Out Transition

You may have noticed that the above transition region's shapes are different compared to the first example. The arrow-shaped regions indicate manual transitions—the arrow is actually a handle to drag left or right to adjust the transition's duration.

To change a manual transition's duration:

Drag the left or right-hand end (as shown below) of the transition region to stretch or shrink it, or specify an absolute value in the transition's Properties pane.

Remember that each transition takes time to happen—so make sure the video in the overlap region is not part of the main action. If you expect to use transitions, it's a good idea to allow a couple of seconds of non-essential material at the start and end of clips when you initially capture them.

 The duration of Automatic transitions is altered automatically by moving either clip on the timeline.

To replace transitions:

1. Select one or more In or Out transitions on the timeline, i.e.

    - For specific transitions, **Ctrl**-click on each clip's transition region one-by-one. This can be carried out across multiple tracks if needed.

    - For all transitions on a single track, select any single transition on the track, then press **Ctrl+A**.

    - For all transitions across multiple tracks, select a transition on each of the tracks (with **Ctrl**-click), then press **Ctrl+A**.

2. Click **Transition Gallery** on the context toolbar.

3. From the dialog, choose a category from the upper window. In the lower window, review the presets available (their names indicate their intended function). Select a preset, e.g. 3D Page Roll.

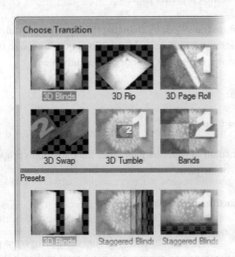

4. Click **OK**.

The Transition name(s) changes, e.g. from "Cross-Fade" to "3D Page Roll":

The end of the first clip is indicated by the vertical dashed red line.

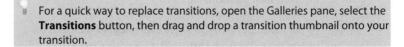

For a quick way to replace transitions, open the Galleries pane, select the **Transitions** button, then drag and drop a transition thumbnail onto your transition.

Modifying transitions

Transitions added to your project will have their own set of properties associated with them. These are highly customizable via the **Properties** pane, just like any other object in MoviePlus. Try selecting a transition region and check its properties in the Properties pane.

The ability to customize transitions by changing these property settings means that the presets supplied are merely a starting point for you to further create and save your own transitions to your own requirements.

To modify a transition:

1. Select the transition region.

2. From the transition's Properties pane, alter the transition's properties at the bottom of the pane.

To save a modified transition to a new name:

○ Click the [Add to Gallery] button at the top of the Properties pane. Once named, the transition appears as a new preset in the Choose Transition dialog.

Adjusting transition properties

A transition, when applied, possesses a single keyframe which dictates the transition duration, interpolation, and settings particular to the type of transition, e.g. blur, transition direction, etc. This applies a uniform setting throughout the transition's duration.

A single keyframe is shown in a Transition strip, shown directly below the clip when double-clicking the transition region (double-click again to hide the strip). In and Out transitions are shown in separate strips with your chosen transition already selected. For example, for an automatic In transition "3D Page Roll" and manual Out transition "Iris Wipe" applied to a single clip:

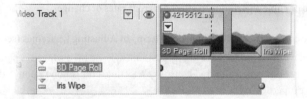

By clicking on the keyframe (the button on each strip) on either transition, the properties of the transition can be modified for the duration of the transition (you alter each keyframe's properties in the Properties pane). The duration of automatic transitions cannot be modified.

If one keyframe is modified the change is applied over the transition's duration. However, more exciting transitions can be made by changing your transition over time.

Applying transitions over time

It is possible to specify how a transition alters throughout its duration by setting keyframes at different points on its strip, but only within the transition's duration (and not over a whole clip or track). The strip allows keyframes to be place along its length, which can be modified in turn to define how a transition's properties are to be applied at that point in the transition. The 3D Page Roll transition above could have a second keyframe (with different properties) added at the end of the transition, to allow the transition to change over time, i.e.

During video preview, as the time indicator passes along the timeline the video's transition will change over time by using the differing properties of the last visited keyframe and the next keyframe on the timeline. The transition can be interpolated linearly or can adopt different types of quadratic or cubic algorithms to effect different rates of change.

Keyframe control is described in general terms in Adjusting keyframes (see p. 98).

Snapping

If **Snapping** is enabled (Arrange menu), the transition will conveniently fit into the overlap region. If snapping is disabled, or you drag the transition to an overlapping area between tracks, it will adopt a default overlap time as set in **Tools>Options>Editing**. Any applied transition should always match the overlap region, i.e. where two clips are co-existing on the timeline.

Whren snapping is enabled, your clips will be "sticky" when you drag clips near the default overlap period (MoviePlus offers a 1-second sticky overlap point by default). This makes it easy to keep a standard transition duration throughout your project without manually editing each transition duration in the Properties pane (or very carefully dragging your clips) for each overlap; MoviePlus uses standard values which you can alter in the **Tools>Options>Editing** dialog. The overlap value is also used as a default transition duration when you add multiple image clips to the timeline simultaneously—great for making quick slide shows!

Using markers

Markers have several uses in MoviePlus but are always added along the top of your timeline at the current time indicator. Three types of marker are available:

▷ Marker 1   **Basic marker**
Used as simple reference points, to indicate important events occurring at key times in your movie, e.g. sound or action, or to mark the start and end of clips on more complex multi-track projects (for positioning and arranging).

▢ Chapter 1   **Chapter point**
For use exclusively in DVD or VCD creation. These indicate the beginning of chapters when creating menus for DVDs (see Menu Designer: Editing chapter properties on p. 192).

◢ Selection Start   **Selection markers**
Define a time range for selective pre-rendering
◣ Selection End   or to export only part of your MoviePlus project (to file, PSP, or iPod).

Markers of any type can be added at any point on your timeline—they can be labelled, repositioned by dragging, as well as navigated.

To insert a marker:

1. Click on the timeline ruler to set the time indicator's position.

2. From the context toolbar's ▷ Marker ⌄ drop-down list choose:

   ● **Insert Marker**.
   OR

   ● **Insert Chapter Point**.
   OR

   ● **Set Selection Start** (or **End**).

By default, markers will be named according to type, i.e. Marker 1, Marker 2, Chapter 1, Chapter 2, Selection Start, etc.

To select a marker:

   ● Click the marker box (whether a basic marker, chapter point, or selection marker) on the timeline ruler (use **Shift**-click to select multiple markers).

To rename your marker:

   ● Go to the selected marker's Properties pane and edit the **Marker** field.

To delete a marker:

   ● Click on the marker and press **Delete**.

Navigating markers

If you're working on a long timeline you may need to navigate your markers so you can check that each marker is of the correct type and position. The navigation method is the same for any marker type (basic, chapter point, or selection marker).

To navigate markers one by one:

- With any marker selected, use **Shift**+left or **Shift**+right arrow keys

To navigate markers via dialog:

- Use 🔲 **Go to Marker...** on the Transport menu to select from markers (of any type) listed in a dialog.

Using chapter points

Chapter points are a type of marker used to define where chapters play from in your generated DVD—much the same as the initial menu shown in any Movie DVD from your local movie store. In the Menu Designer, chapter points inserted in your timeline will be detected and the associated chapters will be thumb nailed automatically (see Menu Designer on p. 187).

> 🏳 Insert Chapter In Storyboard mode, chapter points can be inserted at the start of any clip using the **Insert Chapter** button on the Storyboard toolbar.

If you want to convert a basic marker to a chapter point, simply select **chapter point** in the selected marker's Properties pane, and set the additional chapter point options as required.

Options let you control the chapter end action expected once the DVD chapter has finished playing in your DVD player. If the **Progress to next chapter** is enabled the next chapter is played automatically. Alternatively, the **Return to title menu** option keeps your chapters independent of each other, by returning to the menu once the chapter has played. This latter option would be useful if your DVD is to contain separate unrelated movies.

As an example of chapter points on the timeline, a climbing movie could have named chapter points which represent key points on the movie, e.g. Teamwork, Effort, etc.

When you decide to create your disc, these named chapters will be shown as thumbnails that can be clicked to play the movie from that point.

Using selection markers

Selection markers differ slightly from basic markers and chapter points. Instead, they work as a pair to set a time range on your timeline within which MoviePlus can perform operations limited to that set range. Operations include:

- Pre-rendering part of the timeline that contains complex MoviePlus-applied effects and transitions, for improved preview playback.

- Exporting a part of your movie by setting an export range. Used for exporting to file, PSP, or iPod.

To limit to a specific time range:

1. Click on the timeline ruler to set the time indicator's position.

2. From the context toolbar's ▷ Marker drop-down menu, choose **Set Selection Start** (or right-click on the time indicator) to set the start of your time range. From the same menu, select **Set Selection End** to set the end of your range.

3. (Optional) Drag your ▶ Selection Start and ◀ Selection End markers along the timeline to fine-tune your time range.

Once set, any pre-rendering or exporting will be limited to the chosen time range. Pre-rendering is carried out with the **Pre-render Selected Range** option (Preview menu).

Looping

When you are manipulating clips on your timeline, it is extremely easy to make audio or video clips loop or repeat themselves. Like trimming, you will most probably find that looping, freeze-frames (static extensions), or the speeding up or slowing down of audio and video are common tasks. Other kinds of clips, such as image or text clips, can all have their duration changed but do not loop or repeat.

As an example of looping, a short audio clip of crowd noise can be repeated (by looping the part of the audio clip) for the duration of the accompanying video clip to artificially prolong the length of that audio clip.

To loop a clip:

1. Select an audio or video clip.

2. (Optional) For looping to a precise time, set the time indicator's position on the timeline beyond the end of the clip end.

3. From the Properties pane, check **Enable Clip Extending** and ensure the **Loop** radio button is enabled.

4. To set the number of loops, simply grab one end of the clip on the timeline using your mouse and drag it outwards, making the clip longer. If dragging the right edge, the clip will begin "playing" again after its original end point. If dragging the left edge, the clip will end and restart at its original start point.

    As your clip is extended, you will see small yellow markers along the bottom of the clip; these indicate the repetitions or loops. In the audio sample below, we've stretched the right edge of an audio clip until it is looped and will play fully five times.

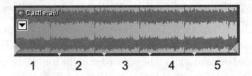

For looped video clips, black triangles along the top of the clip will indicate the position of the "poster frame" previews.

 If you want to trim a "looping" clip, the looping frames will update to reflect the new In or Out point after retrimming.

Looping with trimmed clips

To gain a direct appreciation of the length of the clip on the timeline, the clip's "trimmed" In and Out points, and what portion of the clip is being repeated, you can reveal the clip's strip by clicking **In/Out Points** on the clip's Attributes menu (select ▼ on a clip).

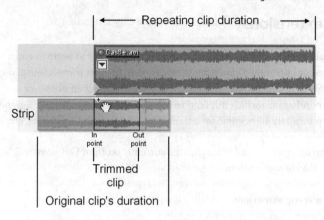

In the example above, the displayed **strip** allows for some fine editing. The audio clip has been trimmed in length by dragging both the left and right edges inwards. The section labelled "Trimmed clip" represents the duration of the trimmed media—the shaded regions left and right of the trim region represent unwanted original audio. The right-edge of the trimmed clip was then dragged to the right after **Enable Clip Extending** was set to **Loop**.

You do not need to reveal the strip to be able to perform the loop operation, but it may help you see which section of a trimmed clip is being repeated when working with trimmed clips.

Time shifting

You can change which section of your original video clip is being played within the trimmed region, without altering the position of your trimmed clip on the timeline, by dragging the hand cursor left or right in the trimmed clip's region. You can imagine that the trimmed region is a small window that can only "see" a small region of the landscape of your video. The drag we've described means you can move left or right to change your view, leaving the window where it is; this has the effect of shifting the trimmed video's in- and out-points relative to the original video clip.

Static extensions

Also called freeze-frame, a static extension is a useful way to begin or end a trimmed or untrimmed clip. A static extension of the first frame could allow for a fade in or other transition, a zoom to give the subject emphasis, or a background against which titles can be overlaid. A static extension at the end of a clip similarly allows time for a transition, a background for credits, etc.

If you're using a trimmed video clip, the currently set In or Out point will be used as the static extension.

To apply a static extension:

1. Select an audio or video clip.

2. (Optional) For precise extensions, set the time indicator's position on the timeline beyond the end of the clip end.

3. From the Properties pane, check **Enable Clip Extending** and ensure the **Static** radio button is enabled.

4. Hover over either end of you clip until you see a ⟨▥▥▥ or ▥▥▥⟩ cursor, then drag your clip's end outwards to make it longer. If dragging the right edge, the clip will "freeze" the final frame. If dragging the left edge, the clip will freeze the first frame.

As your clip is extended, you will see a small yellow marker under the clip (circled below) indicating the original start or end point of your clip before your static extension was applied. The black triangles along the top of the clip merely indicate the position of the "poster frame" previews.

Slowing down and speeding up

Video clips can be slowed down (slow motion) or speeded up by decreasing or increasing the **Play speed** on the clip's Properties pane. You'll see the duration change on the chosen clip as you adjust this value—when a video plays slower or faster, it has a longer or shorter duration, respectively. Image or text clips cannot have their **Play speed** adjusted.

Masking

Masks are a way of using an image to "cut out" a rectangular or other-shaped portion from a video, leaving transparency around the subject, effectively removing a background to give focus to a foreground element. You can also use masks to crop video, for multiple picture-in-picture effects, popularized by comic-book superhero movies. Masks can remove a foreground element to reveal another video or image clip through the cut-out region (e.g., you can create a mask which cuts a hole in a picture, perhaps in the shape of a sports stadium big-screen, so your image or video would display where the screen-shaped cutout is).

Masks as used in MoviePlus are best created as transparent images with a white region to indicate the shape of underlying video to keep; the white region is like the inside shape of a cookie cutter, the transparent region is discarded like the outlying pastry around your cutter. You can also use images that contain a mixture of different colours and transparent regions for advanced masking.

In addition, QuickShapes let you apply shaped masks directly onto the timeline with no fuss. See Using CG clips on p. 60.

You can create your own masks with Serif PhotoPlus.

You can see the result of combining a QuickShape "heart" mask with a video clip, each stored on separate video tracks.

Original video

**Mask QuickShape applied
over video on different tracks**

**Resulting composition only
has a specific (mask-shaped)
region**

Video tracks

Before you go ahead and add a mask to your timeline, it's useful to know in advance how masks and the organization of your video tracks work together. Masks need to occupy a track of their own to have an affect on underlying video compositions... the mask's white regions determine which regions of underlying video clips you see—the mask sits on top of other video clips to act as a virtual cookie cutter.

Using the Mask blend mode

Masking is made possible by the correct arrangement of tracks (as described above), but also by the setting of the Mask track's **Blend Mode**. When set to "**Mask**", the Blend Mode on the top-most track in your project will affect transparency on tracks below it.

Restricting mask effects with video groups

To limit which tracks are affected (the depth to which the cookie cutter actually cuts), you can store the mask track with blend mode applied (and other video tracks you want affected) within a Video Group, leaving other video tracks you do not want affected outside the group.

Looking at the track names in the example below, "Holiday Track 2" is not subject to the heart-shaped clipping that the Mask Track is performing because it is outside the video group—the mask's effect is limited to tracks within its video group, i.e. the Main Holiday Track only.

The Main Holiday Track footage is masked as it is in the same group as Mask Track; Holiday Track 2 is kept outside Video Group 1.

The mask only cuts out content from the image of the dolphin. The underlying video, outside of the video group, is unaffected by the masking operation!

Creating your own masks

To create a mask it is recommended you use a bitmap (photo) editing program that fully supports transparency, such as Serif PhotoPlus. Some other programs that can easily create shapes with or without soft edges (and can export images with transparency, such as 32-bit PNG) are also useful for creating masks—Serif DrawPlus is an example.

You should aim to use white to create the region you wish to maintain in your video, and transparency for the areas you wish to cut away. Partial transparency is supported, so you can create regions of translucency as well as using a mask to create solid regions of opacity and transparency in your video.

Remember to create your masks at a suitable size for your project, taking pixel aspect ratio into account. For the majority of output formats, MoviePlus creates non-square (rectangular) pixels at export time: your DVD video in PAL regions, for instance, is created at 720 pixels wide, but after pixel stretching (as carried out by DVD players and the MoviePlus Video Preview pane) the video is stretched to the equivalent of 787 pixel wide (655 pixels wide in the case of NTSC). The pixel aspect ratio for DVD PAL is 1.0926 and this is the factor by which the video is affected by stretching (mask images need to be wider than the project size by the same factor). As a quick guide, you should multiply the project's pixel aspect ratio x frame width = width you need to create your mask.

To add your own masks to your project, browse to their saved location using the Media pane, and drag your mask image onto a track of its own, positioned above the video you would like to mask.

Once in your project, you can also stretch your mask to fit using **Stretch** from the **Fit** drop-down menu on the Timeline context toolbar. Alternatively, you can always adjust size and position using a transform envelope (see p. 94).

Blue screening (Chroma Key)

The blue screening process, referred to as **chroma key** in MoviePlus, enjoys a few other names including colour keying, matting, green-screening, and colour separation overlay. It is a method of removing a colour (or a colour range) from one video or image to reveal another video or image behind it. The "removed" colour becomes transparent.

This process is commonly used for weather broadcasts and of course in many movie blockbusters. To start with, the foreground subject—a weather presenter for instance—is filmed against a solid-coloured and evenly-illuminated backdrop. Using MoviePlus (or expensive studio wizardry in the case of live TV weather slots), the solid coloured region of this video can be made transparent using a Chroma Key effect, revealing an underlying video. In the case of some weather presenting, the video "behind" the presenter can show a weather map with animated symbols or weather systems.

In movies, the process saves actors being put in dangerous positions, such as visually-stunning explosions, or in places that cannot be reached for practical or budgetary reasons, such as across the other side of the globe or in space.

It's not only a background that can be removed; you can, for instance, hold up a solid-coloured card while being filmed and later remove that solid colour from the video to create a card-shaped cut-out. The alternate "background" video would then display through this "hole".

Blue screening in action

Simple blue-screen filming of a hand against a solid-coloured background, a wooden frame with blue cloth stretched over it in this case.

Background video, placed on the track below the blue-screen footage on the timeline.

The upper video clip on the timeline, the blue-screen footage, has had a Chroma Key effect applied to it. Properties sliders were adjusted to remove all the blue.

Applying the Chroma Key effect

Effects in MoviePlus can be applied to individual video clips, whole tracks, or video groups. While Chroma Key can also be applied to all three hierarchies, it is most commonly used with individual video clips, as it is not usual for there to be multiple clips with the same background colour to be made transparent.

The effect is applied like any other video effect, from the [⌕ Effects] button on the Timeline context toolbar (see Applying video effects on p. 135).

The Chroma Key effect will automatically remove whichever colour is associated with the Chroma Key effect applied to your video. For example, if you use the "Blue screen" preset then the preset's colour (RGB 0,0,255) is removed if present in your video clip. You'll more than likely need to accurately make your effect colour to be the same as your blue screening backdrop colour:

To change the Chroma Key colour:

1. Display the Chroma Key effect's Properties pane.

2. Either:

     ○ Use the colour picker pipette to select a new colour value from the upper clip that you want to remove (hold down the mouse button, and drag the pipette over the colour you require, and release). This could be the backdrop colour.
       OR

     ○ Define a new colour by clicking the **Colour** spectrum and, from the Adjust Colour dialog, select an RGB, HSL or HTML code.

Changing thresholds and blurring

MoviePlus lets you fine-tune the Chroma Key effect to help the colour-detection processes determine which bits of your video to make transparent. It is very useful to be able to set a **Low** and **High** threshold for colour detection—this transparency is set according to brightness levels. **Blur** lets you blur the shape of the transparent region generated by the Chroma Key effect.

Changing the Chroma Key effect over time

You can adjust the Chroma Key settings so that they change over time, perhaps to account for a change in lighting conditions that affects the colour you're trying to remove. Your Chroma Key effect can start by removing pale blue and slowly change to removing a stronger blue, for instance.

For more information, see Adjusting keyframes on p. 98.

Video overlays

You can "layer" all sorts of different kinds of clips on top of existing video or image clips—this flexibility opens up a world of possibilities in your video production.

Overlays, in basic terms, are two or more clips being displayed at once, one on top of the other—these clips are layered on multiple video tracks. For the bottom clip to still be visible despite having another clip on top of it, the top clip needs to:

- be smaller than the bottom clip.

- have transparent regions.

- have reduced opacity.

The principle can be understood with a festive example of an image overlay over a video clip.

What is on display underneath your overlay depends on the structure of your timeline. The example above shows a two-track project. The Christmas overlay graphic exists on top of the underlying video clip for as long as the image overlay exists above the lower clip.

Top clip made smaller

When you add an opaque clip to the upper track so that it is displayed on top of other clips, it is likely to occlude them completely or almost completely, blocking out the clip below so all you can see is the content of the top-most track. To resize your top clip so you can see "around it" to underlying clips, use a transform envelope on the upper clip or track (see p. 94). You can also reshape your clip, deform with perspective (as shown above) and you can even animate the resizing/reshaping process (see online Help).

Top clip has transparent regions

Overlaid STV video

Serif ImpactPlus or DrawPlus can be used to export as **Serif Transparent Video** (STV), creating animations that make for compelling effects in your movies, including smoke, fire, ethereal mists, sparkling fireworks (for ImpactPlus) and impressive Flash-based designs (for DrawPlus; export as keyframe animation). If you own either Serif product see its online Help for information about exporting; remember to choose the STV format if you want your export to have a transparent background!

When you add an STV video file to a track above existing video or images, you do not need to take any further action, MoviePlus will smoothly overlay the STV on top of the video, colour or image on the lower track, revealing underlying clips through the video's transparent region(s).

Overlaid images

Images overlaid on tracks above other images or video can make for some fun projects (like the Christmas example above). If the image on the top track has built-in transparency you will automatically be able to see through the transparent region to the underlying clips.

There may be more than one way you can achieve your effect—e.g., a picture of a billboard advertising poster displaying your video within the billboard area can be achieved by either placing your video above a billboard image and shaping the video to match the billboard area using a transform envelope, or you can also cut out the billboard region of the image using a photo-editing program such as Serif's PhotoPlus (exported as a 32-bit PNG to maintain transparency) and place it on top of your video, perhaps shaping your underlying video to approximately match the billboard region, again using a transform envelope. Both methods would have similar results; the second would allow some foreground objects in the image, such as a street sign, to sit in front of the billboard (see below).

Top clip with reduced opacity

There are a number of ways to reduce opacity of upper clips to partially reveal underlying clips—the quickest is to adjust overall track opacity using the **Opacity** slider in the selected Video track's Properties pane.

You can also adjust the opacity of a track (or even the clip itself) over time by manipulating its opacity envelope and associated keyframes. See Using envelopes and Adjusting keyframes on p. 94 and p. 98 to learn how to modify envelopes by making keyframe adjustments.

Introducing transforms

Transforms allow you to resize your clips within the overall project size (which helps achieve picture-in-picture effects), to add perspective, and to scroll video, image and CG clips (Backgrounds and QuickShapes) in any direction.

The possibilities are almost endless, because not only can you transform individual clips, you can also transform entire video tracks and even collections of video tracks in video groups.

Several key techniques use transforms—here's a quick summary, using the above examples for reference.

Scaling   This has been used in the second and third examples above; each video clip started at full screen size.

Motion   Motion can be used, e.g. to position the text to the left in the first sample, and is illustrated by combining rotation and scaling in the third sample. Transform settings can collude to create video animation.

Perspective	Perspective has been applied to the "seaview" video in the first sample above.
Picture-in-picture effects	This is used in the third sample above; the group of four videos is smaller than the background video so is "picture-in-picture". It combines scaling and a new position, either static or animated.

Transforms all involve manipulation of MoviePlus's transform envelope, which you'll find discussed in Using envelopes (see p. 94). For more information, you could consult the online Help or the **Timeline Techniques** section in the MoviePlus X3 Director's Guide, where such transforming techniques are covered in greater detail.

Effects

5

Effects

Applying video effects

Effects can add variety and visual excitement to a video (or image) clip. Some effects, like **Brightness/Contrast** or **Gamma**, are designed to correct the original image; others, like **Filter Effects**, **Mosaic** or **Diffuse Glow**, are simply special effects.

The supported special effects are described as follows (See also effects for colour correction on p. 145):

- **Chroma Key** - A method of removing a colour (or a colour range) from one video to reveal another video or image behind it. The "removed" colour becomes transparent.

- **Colourize** - Offers an easy way to apply a colour tint/wash.

- **Diffuse Glow** - This broadens highlights in the video by brightening gradually outward from existing highlights.

- **Emboss** - The Emboss effect remaps contours to simulate a bas-relief effect. This creates a convex rounded edge and shadow effect.

- **Filter Effects** - Filter Effects encompass Shadows, Glows, Bevels, Emboss, Colour fills and 3D special effects. Apply individually or in combination in a highly configurable design environment.

- **Gaussian Blur** - The Gaussian Blur effect smoothes the image or video by averaging pixels. It's especially useful for removing a moiré (interference) pattern from scanned images and can help regions of visual interference from fine patterns.

- **Gradient Map** - The Gradient Map adjustment is for remapping lightness information in the clip to a new colour range. It makes for great "posterized" effects and is a quick substitute where a pop-art feel is being sought.

- **Greyscale** - This effect creates shades of grey; monotones ranging from black through to white.

- **Invert** - This effect inverts the colours, in the same way that a photo and its negative are opposites of each other.

- **Mask** - The Mask effect is a useful way to convert a clip into a more suitable mask by adjusting its lightness or other tonal values.

- **Mosaic** - The Mosaic effect creates blocks of uniform colour for a tiled appearance.

- **Motion Blur** - Exaggerate motion in your video clip, by blurring object movement.

- **Noise** - The Noise effect adds graininess.

- **Old Film** - Use the effect to simulate vintage movies; control ageing and movie quality.

- **Solarize** - The Solarize effect is similar to a Negative Image function, but lets you set the threshold value above which colours can be inverted. (Solarization is a darkroom technique in which a partially developed image is re-exposed to light, producing dramatic changes in mid-tone regions).

- **Threshold** - The Threshold effect creates a harsh duo-tone black and white image, with no blend through shades of grey.

- **Unsharp Mask** - Unlike many sharpening tools that affect the entire clip, the Unsharp Mask effect works mainly at edges. It's excellent for improving clip quality.

Audio special effects (see p. 147) can also be applied to audio clips.

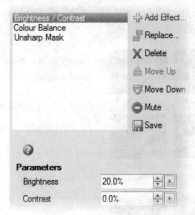

Individual or cumulative effects can be managed from an Effects tab. They can be added, replaced, deleted, and rearranged all from this tab. Applied effects are shown in an effect list; effects at the top of the list are applied to the clip first. When selected, effects' properties can be adjusted directly in the pane. Any modified effect can be saved for future use.

Applying effects

To apply an effect:

1. Select the clip on the storyboard (or timeline).

2. Click the **Effects** button on the context toolbar.

3. From the Properties pane (Effects tab), click the **Add Effect...** button.

4. From the dialog, choose a category (see explanations above) from the upper window. In the lower window, review the presets available (especially their names, which indicate their intended function). Select a preset.

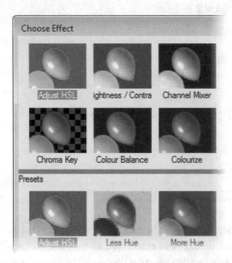

5.   Click **OK**. The effect is added to the Effects tab's effects list.

💡 ✏ In Storyboard mode, a clip's thumbnail with an effect applied will show a symbol. Click the symbol to view applied effects.

💡 🖊 For a quick way to apply effects, open the Galleries pane, select the **Effects** button, then drag and drop a chosen preset onto your clip.

Any effect added to your project will have its own set of properties associated with it. The effect's properties can be altered in the Properties pane (Effects tab).

To modify an effect:

1.   Select the clip.

2.   From the Properties pane (Effects tab), choose the effect to be edited from the effects list.

3.   Alter the effects' properties at the bottom of the tab.

To save a modified effect to a new name:

- Click the [Save] button in the Properties pane (Effects tab). Once named, the effect appears as a new preset (in the Choose Effect dialog) next time you want to apply an effect.

2D filter effects

MoviePlus provides a variety of **filter effects** that you can use to transform any clip. "3D" filter effects let you create the impression of a textured surface and are covered elsewhere (see p. 142). Here we'll look at 2D filter effects exclusively. The following examples show each 2D filter effect when applied to the letter "A."

Drop Shadow	Inner Shadow	Outer Glow	Inner Glow
Inner Bevel	Outer Bevel	Emboss	Pillow Emboss
Gaussian Blur	Zoom Blur	Radial Blur	Motion Blur
Colour Fill	Feather	Outline	

To apply 2D filter effects:

1. Select a video or image clip and click the [Effects] button on the context toolbar, then from the Properties pane (Effects tab), click the **Add Effect...** button.

2. From the Choose Effect dialog, select the **Filter Effects** category and choose a preset from the lower window.

3. Click **OK**.

To edit a filter effect:

1. From the Properties pane (Effects tab), select "Filter Effects" in the effects list and click the **Edit Effects...** button. The **Filter Effects** dialog is displayed.

2. (Optional) If needed, expand the preview pane by clicking the ▷ **Show/Hide Preview** button. When expanded, the effects are applied only in the preview window. While the pane is collapsed (click the button again), filter effects are applied directly to the clip.

3. To apply a particular effect, check its box in the list at left.

4. To adjust the properties of a specific effect, select its name and vary the dialog controls. Adjust the sliders or enter specific values to vary the combined effect. (You can also select a slider and use the keyboard arrows.) Options differ from one effect to another.

5. Click **OK** to apply the effect or **Cancel** to abandon changes.

Creating outlines

MoviePlus lets you create a coloured outline around objects, especially text and shapes (as a **filter effect**). For any outline, you can set the outline width, colour fill, transparency, and blend mode. The outline can also take a gradient fill, a unique **contour** fill (fill runs from the inner to outer edge of the outline width), or pattern fill and can also sit inside, outside, or be centred on the object edge.

As with all effects you can switch the outline effect on and off. You'll be able to apply a combination of 2D or 3D filter effects along with your outline, by checking other options in the Filter Effects dialog.

Blur

Various blur effects can be applied to MoviePlus objects. The types of blur include:

- **Gaussian**: the effect smoothes by averaging pixels using a weighted curve.

- **Zoom**: applies converging streaks to the image to simulate a zoom lens.

- **Radial**: applies concentric streaks to the object to simulate a rotating camera or subject.

- **Motion**: applies straight streaks to the object to simulate the effect of camera or subject movement.

3D filter effects

3D filter effects create the impression of a textured surface on the clip, track or group itself. You can apply one or more effects to the same clip—3D Bump Map, 3D Pattern Map, and 3D Lighting are all available. Some impressive effects can be achieved on a whole range of objects, particularly Text, Background and QuickShape clips.

 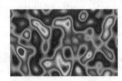

Overview

To apply 3D filter effects:

1. Select a video or image clip and click the button on the context toolbar, then from the Properties pane (Effects tab), click the **Add Effect...** button.

2. From the Choose Effect dialog, select the **Filter Effects** category and choose a 3D preset from the lower window.

3. Click **OK**.

To edit a filter effect:

1. From the Properties pane (Effects tab), select "Filter Effects" in the effects list and click the **Edit Effects...** button. The **Filter Effects** dialog is displayed.

2. (Optional) If needed, expand the preview pane by clicking the ▷ **Show/Hide Preview** button. When expanded, the effects are applied only in the preview window. While the pane is collapsed (click the button again), filter effects are applied directly to the clip.

3. Check the **3D Effects** box in the list (unless you've already selected a 3D preset). The **3D Lighting** box is checked by default.

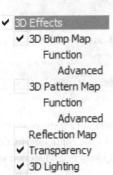

3D Effects is a master switch for this group, and its settings of **Blur** and **Depth** make a great difference; you can click the "+" button to unlink them for independent adjustment.

3D Lighting provides a "light source" without which any depth information in the effect wouldn't be visible. The lighting settings let you illuminate your 3D landscape and vary its reflective properties.

4. Once **3D Effects** is enabled (see Overview), adjust the "master control" sliders here to vary the overall properties of any individual 3D effects you select, i.e.

    • **Blur** specifies the amount of smoothing applied. Larger blur sizes give the impression of broader, more gradual changes in height.

    • **Depth** specifies how steep the changes in depth appear.

    • The ⊞ button is normally down, which links the two sliders so that sharp changes in Depth are smoothed out by the Blur parameter. To adjust the sliders independently, click the button so it's up.

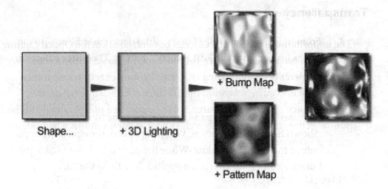

Shape...   + 3D Lighting   + Bump Map

+ Pattern Map

You can combine multiple 3D filter effects, as in the illustration above. The effects are applied cumulatively.

The procedures for applying 3D Filter Effects are covered in the MoviePlus Help but here's a quick review of each effect type.

3D bump map

The **3D Bump Map** effect creates the impression of a textured surface by applying a mathematical function you select to add depth information, for a peak-and-valley effect. You can use 3D Bump Map in conjunction with one or more additional 3D filter effects.

3D pattern map

The **3D Pattern Map** effect creates the impression of a textured surface by applying a mathematical function you select to introduce colour variations. You can use 3D Pattern Map in conjunction with one or more other 3D filter effects.

Transparency

The uniform transparency of a clip can be controlled via the **Opacity** setting
in the clip's properties. However, for more sophisticated transparency
control, especially for simulating reflective lighting effects, transparency
settings can instead be set within the 3D filter effects dialog (check the
Transparency option). Transparency can be adjusted independently for both
non-reflective surfaces (typically a clip's edge shadows shown when side-lit)
and top-lit surfaces.

3D reflection map

The **3D Reflection Map** effect is used to simulate mirrored surfaces by
selection of a pattern (i.e., a bitmap which possesses a shiny surface) which
"wraps around" a selected clip. Patterns which simulate various realistic
indoor and outdoor environments can be adopted, with optional use of 3D
lighting to further reflect off the clips' edges.

3D lighting

The **3D Lighting** effect works in conjunction with other 3D effects to let you
vary the surface illumination and reflective properties.

Colour correction

MoviePlus offers a wide variety of colour adjustment presets that you can
apply to clips. These adjustments—to brightness, contrast, hue, and so on—
are normally carried out on clips, as most deficiencies will be inherited from
the recording of the clip (e.g., over-exposure, poor weather conditions, etc.).

Colour correction effects are applied and managed in the same way as for any
other effect, i.e. go to the Properties pane (Effects tab), choose Add Effect,
then choose a category then effect from the effects gallery. Use the effect's
Properties pane to alter the adjustment settings. See Applying Effect on
p. 137 for more information.

Let's take a look at the colour adjustment effect categories in turn.

Adjust HSL	Hue, Saturation, and Lightness (HSL) are components of a standard colour model that's used to identify colours. Generally speaking, Hue refers to the colour's tint—what most of us think of as rainbow or spectrum colours with name associations, like "blue" or "magenta." Saturation describes the colour's purity—a totally unsaturated video has only greys. Lightness is what we intuitively understand as relative darkness or lightness—ranging from full black at one end to full white at the other. Adjust HSL lets you alter these components independently.
Brightness / Contrast	Brightness refers to overall lightness or darkness, while contrast describes the tonal range, or spread between lightest and darkest values. This is a "quick and dirty" way of correcting a clip, for example one that was over-exposed or under-exposed.
Channel Mixer	The Channel Mixer adjustment lets you adjust each separate colour channel (Red, Green, or Blue) using a mix of all the current colour channels.
Colour Balance	The Colour Balance adjustment lets you adjust colour balance for general colour correction in the clip. Combinations of Cyan/Red, Magenta/Green and Yellow/Blue can be adjusted to lower or raise each colour mix.
Curves	The Curves adjustment lets you correct the tonal range of a clip—the spread of lightness values through shadow, midtone, and highlight regions—and control individual colour components.

Gamma	The Gamma adjustment lets you adjust the amount of mid-tone brightness in your clip. Think of midtones as the grey shading that lie between shadows and highlights present throughout your clip.
Levels	The Levels adjustment lets you emphasize mid-tone lightness regions in each or all of the three primary video colours, red, green, and blue.

Applying audio effects

In the same way that you can apply video effects to video clips, you can apply audio effects to audio clips also. In fact the process of applying and editing effects is identical for both—MoviePlus treats them equally.

Audio effects range from more commonly encountered effects such as Bass and Reverb, to more technical effects such as Low, High Pass, Compressor, Expander, and many more.

Whichever effect you want to apply you'll need to have recorded, captured, or imported your audio file in advance; the file must also be present as a clip on your storyboard or timeline. Once present, the clip can have an effect applied.

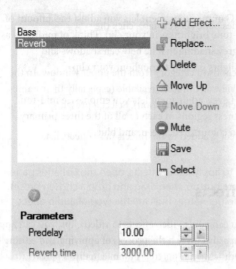

Individual or cumulative audio effects can be managed from an Effects tab on the Properties pane. They can be added, replaced, deleted, and rearranged all from this tab. Applied effects are shown in an effect list; effects at the top of the list are applied to the clip first. When selected, an effects' properties can be adjusted directly in the pane. Any modified effect can be saved for future use.

In Timeline mode, an audio effect can be equally applied to an audio track or group, as well as an audio clip. This will influence the audio of a clip on the same track or group.

Applying audio effects

To apply an effect:

1. Select the audio clip on the storyboard (or clip, track, or group on the timeline).

2. Click the ⟨ Effects button on the context toolbar.

3. From the Properties pane (Effects tab), click the ⊕ Add Effect... button.

4. From the dialog, choose a category from the upper window. In the lower window, review any presets available (especially their names, which indicate their intended function). Select a preset.

5. Click **OK**. The effect is added to the Effects tab's effects list.

💡 🔲 For a quick way to apply audio effects, open the Galleries pane, select the **Audio Effects** button, then drag and drop a chosen preset onto your audio. The folder names indicate the type of audio effect available.

Any effect added to your project will have its own set of properties associated with it. The effect's properties can be altered in the Properties pane (Effects tab).

To modify an audio effect:

1. Select the audio clip, track or group which has the effect applied.

2. From the Properties pane (Effects tab), choose the effect to be edited from the effects list.

3. Alter the effects' properties at the bottom of the tab.

To save a modified effect to a new name:

● Click the 🔲 Save button in the Properties pane (Effects tab). Once named, the effect appears as a new preset (in the Choose Effect dialog) next time you want to apply an effect.

Using third-party effects

While MoviePlus is packed with a range of preset audio effects you can also adopt third-party **plug-in VST effects** (up to V2.4). If you've already downloaded such effects independently of MoviePlus you can make them appear in your Galleries pane by copying them to the MoviePlus install sub-folder called "VST". You'll need to do this before running MoviePlus. By default, this folder will be C:\Program Files\Serif\MoviePlus\X3\VST\.

The installed VST effects can be applied in exactly the same way as MoviePlus's audio effects—you can adjust their properties in the Properties pane (Effects tab). Note that some more advanced VST effects (ANWIDA Reverb) can be modified with a **VST Properties** button (in the same pane).

You can optionally store your VST effect plug-ins in a folder of your choice, but you'll have to point to this folder via **Tools>Options** (Folders tab) for the effects to show in the Galleries pane.

Installed VST effects are shown in the Effects Gallery in folders named with a [VST] suffix.

Audio

6

Introducing audio

In MoviePlus, it's possible to use audio clips which have been collected by a variety of methods, i.e.

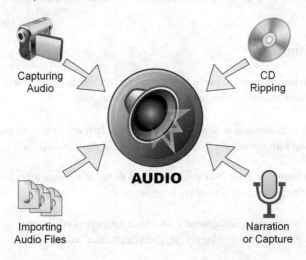

Capturing Audio

CD Ripping

AUDIO

Importing Audio Files

Narration or Capture

- **Capturing audio**: The capture process is capable of capturing just the audio element from a camcorder's combined video/audio input or audio from a microphone (see Capturing video on p. 31).

- **Importing audio files**: You can make use of audio files already on your computer by simply importing them into your project.

- **Recording Narration**: Narrate commentary via microphone as you playback your movie. Narration can play back over existing audio (e.g., a soundtrack).

- **CD Ripping**: Digital ripping of music CDs means that you can adopt your favourite songs as supporting soundtracks in your movie.

Whichever method you choose, audio files will be added to your Media pane. Narration files are also added to the storyboard or timeline automatically (at the time indicator position at which you started recording).

In many instances, the capture or import of a video file to your project will introduce accompanying audio along with your video clip automatically. For instance, capturing via a tape-based camcorder will create an avi file which will contain separate but linked video and audio streams. When you introduce the media file to the storyboard or timeline, the associated audio will follow.

Audio editing

Audio can play an essential part in any movie, and creative audio editing is an art in itself. Standard ingredients of audio might include:

- Production sound as originally recorded (and later captured) "in sync" along with the video, e.g. camcorder footage of your last holiday

- Narration (or voice-over passages) which serves as a commentary or a bridge between sections of your movie.

- Theme music or background sound from a variety of clips, often added as one or more longer clips that run "under" audio narration.

- Sound effects or single-shot audio events, perhaps added for emphasis ("sweetening") or comic relief

If you would like your movie to include more than basic production sound, allow yourself some time to do it right! Skilful sound editing is a combination of technique and judgment. Fortunately, MoviePlus makes the technical part straightforward. Getting sound to coincide properly with the visual track, to come in on cue and end (or fade out) at just the right moment, to blend well with other audio... all are easily accomplished in the Timeline mode.

Adding and replacing audio

Capture001.wav

Audio files can be added to your Media pane in various ways (see Introducing audio on p. 153) and will always show with an audio icon as a thumbnail. If capturing, the default prefix is "Capture".

Once in your project you'll want to add one or more audio files them to either your storyboard or timeline. One exception is when you're recording narration as the narration clip will be added automatically to storyboard or timeline.

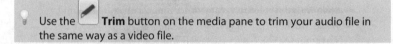

Use the ✏ **Trim** button on the media pane to trim your audio file in the same way as a video file.

Adding audio to the storyboard

If the storyboard is empty, drag your audio clips so that they snap onto horizontal audio or narration strips at the bottom of the storyboard.

You'll see a green strip appear under the thumbnails which indicates the audio clip. The audio clip snaps to the start of any clip.

Capture001.wav

The clip is selectable and as such has its own properties (i.e., Gain and Pan) which can be adjusted (via the Properties pane). See Volume and pan on p. 159.

Adding audio to the timeline

Whenever you add a video clip with an audio component to the timeline, e.g. an AVI file, the audio portion (if present) is automatically added to an available audio track underneath the video track. These two clips maintain a linkage by default, as shown when you select either clip—a strong blue border indicates the current selection, while a paler blue border indicates the linked accompanying clip.

However, when you add a standalone audio file (AVI, WAV, WMA) it can be dragged onto a new or existing audio track.

Audio tracks are managed in much the same way as video tracks, and by the same token, audio clips are managed as for video clips. Please see Adding and arranging tracks and Arranging clips on p. 75 and p. 82, respectively, for more information.

In terms of playback, the audio clip is treated as for a video clip—seek controls can be used, along with trick play and scrubbing.

Audio waveform displays

An audio clip differs from a video clip on the timeline as it doesn't have any poster thumbnails to display. However, the audio clip will display an **Audio Waveform Display** of the audio clip—in other words a visual indication of the audio's dynamic range along the clip's length. The display makes it easy to spot cues and any unforeseen audio events.

Note that the waveform display does not reflect the audio volume, as volume and dynamic range represent two different elements of audio. If you increase the volume the dynamic range does not change (and vice versa).

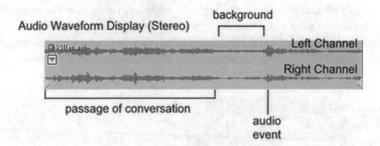

Audio Waveform Display (Stereo)

background

Left Channel

Right Channel

passage of conversation

audio event

The above example shows a stereo waveform display. For a mono waveform display, only a single waveform (channel) is shown.

The waveform display can be hidden by minimizing the audio track—simply click the **Minimize/Restore** button in the track header. Alternatively, switch off the waveform in **Tools>Options>General**. Switch on at any point by right-clicking on the clip and checking **Show Audio Waveforms**.

Audio fading

In a similar way to video in/out transitions, any audio clip can have an audio transition. By default, when overlapping audio clips have been placed on the timeline (normally as a result of adding multiple video clips with accompanying audio clips) an **automatic** transition of type "Fade" is produced between overlapping audio clips. The transition smoothly blends the first clip's audio with the second clip's audio while maintaining the same audio levels throughout the transition's duration.

For non-overlapping audio clips, perhaps at the start or end of the timeline, an **manual** transition can be applied—this fades-in or fades-out an audio clip at the start or end of that clip, respectively. To apply, simply drag the blue triangular handle to the left (shown below) or right to produce the Fade transition. The length of the transition dictates the duration of the fade-in/out.

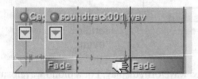

The duration of any manual Fade transition can be changed by dragging its handles or changing the **Duration** value in the transition's Properties pane. An automatic transition's duration can only be changed by moving either clip in relation to the other (the automatic overlap defines the duration).

For automatic or manual transitions, you can adjust the **Interpolation** in the same pane—this alters the rate of change for the progression of the whole transition. The default is Linear, but other settings offer slow and/or fast beginnings and/or ends to the change.

Volume and pan

The Video Preview pane can be used to study project-wide volume and pan settings, and to help you to attain optimum volume and pan—this is just as essential to a well-designed movie project as hours devoted to video editing.

The pane hosts two meters which shows the entire project's **audio levels**. The left and right meters represent the left and right stereo channels, respectively, and report the audio levels in decibels (dB).

The meter levels will increase and decrease according to the volume level at that point in the project's playback.

The concept of the Levels meter is straightforward—the levels will peak and dip according to currently played audio levels. You may have experienced this on music systems while recording.

At some point, the pane may indicate that excessive volume levels are being experienced, i.e. the levels go above 0 on any meter. This is known as **digital clipping** (also known as square wave clipping). It is vital that such clipping does not occur in your project, so you have you set the loudest part of your audio clip to peak below 0 dB (or face audio distortion).

How do you know when clipping occurs? At the top of the example meters opposite, you'll notice two numbers at the top of each meter. The values represent the maximum level or "high-watermark" for each channel if clipping occurs during the current playback. Again using the example, the left channel has at some point during playback peaked at +2.3 dB, while the right channel has peaked at +2.6 dB. You can leave your project to play, then return to check for clipping—if no values appear in red then no clipping has occurred. This saves you from having to watch the entire project's playback!

These values are always reset when playback is restarted.

The pane only gives an accurate indication of incorrectly set audio clips or tracks—whether high or low. The prime objective is therefore to resolve unacceptable volume levels which we'll look at next.

Adjusting volume

Volume adjustment of clips

The volume adjustment on any selected audio clip (or even video clip with audio stream) can be made by altering **Gain** in the object's Properties pane (shown under the **Audio** section). For example, the Gain can be reduced by dragging the slider to the left (from its default 0.0 dB position).

Muting

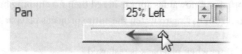 You don't have to delete an audio clip to exclude it from playback. As muting is a property of the clip you can switch **Mute** on and off in the clip's Properties pane. Muting is useful when you might want to temporarily preview your movie without narration, a soundtrack, or a "special effects" audio clip.

Adjusting pan

Adjusting the pan follows the same principles as adjusting volume. The adjustment can be made by altering **Pan** in the object's Properties pane (shown under the **Audio** section). For example, the pan can be reduced by dragging the slider to the left (from its default "Centre" position).

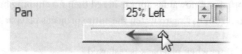

Adding narration

Narration means a passage of speech, normally an accompanying story (or a set of instructions), used to support the visual imagery of a movie.

In MoviePlus, narration (voice-overs) is possible in either Storyboard or Timeline mode, by choosing the point from which to start recording your narration clip (set your time indicator first). As you play back your movie, you record your narration in real-time, then stop recording. The clip is automatically added to the storyboard or timeline, and is also added to the Media pane.

On the storyboard, the narration clip appears under the clip(s) as a purple coloured strip after you've stopped recording.

On the timeline, the narration clip is added from the set time indicator on a Narration track; the track is added automatically.

Setting up your microphone

Two microphone setups are likely: either a separate microphone and stereo headphones, or an integrated microphone in headphones. Devices may connect either via USB or via your computer's sound card (sometimes indirectly from your computer's front panel). Connected devices should be plug-and-play so don't need to be set up manually.

Most headphones are generally equipped with 3.5 mm jack plugs. Check the symbols on the jack plug then match these up with the same symbols on your computer's input sockets.

Consult your microphone documentation and Microsoft Windows for details on how to set up your audio device on your computer.

Recording

The Record Narration dialog lets you alter your recording setup (e.g., microphone clip) and start (and stop) the recording. During recording, a Levels meter indicates the current audio level.

Before recording your narration it's a great idea to bear in mind some useful tips, i.e.

- If you're recording a narration for a specific clip, check the clip's duration in the Properties pane. This will guide you as to how long your narration should last.

- Script what you plan to say, and rehearse your lines! Getting an idea about how long the passage of text is and how it fits in with your movie clip. Be prepared for multiple takes until you're happy.

- Anticipate then remove any possible clips of background noise (dog's barking, traffic noise, TV, radio, etc.)

- You can record more audio than you need to then trim the clip using audio trimming (see p. 37).

- Check your sound levels set in Windows Vista, especially Microphone Boost (shown under Control Panel>Hardware and Sound; Manage audio devices>Recording>Properties>Levels).

To record a narration:

1. Move the time indicator in the Video Preview pane to a chosen recording start point (or select a clip on the storyboard to record from the beginning of that clip).

2. Click the [🎤 Record Narration] button on the Storyboard or Timeline toolbar.

3. From the Record Narration dialog, optionally choose a different **Source** if you have multiple audio input devices, an **Input** (e.g., "Microphone"), or a different audio **Format**.

4. Speak into your microphone to check levels. If the volume is excessive, the Levels meter will show clipping (red areas showing at the top of each meter). To rectify, lower the 🔊 **Master Volume** slider until clipping no longer occurs.

5. Uncheck **Mute audio when recording** if you want existing audio to be played through your computer speakers (and picked up via microphone) as you record. Normally, you'll want to keep this checked to mute your audio as you record (or use headphones), to avoid "echoing".

> Another source of echoing is when the Windows Volume Control outputs the microphone audio through the speakers, so it gets picked up by the microphone again (feedback). Avoid echoing in this case by use of headphones or by muting the microphone output.

6. To start recording, click the **Record** button and begin your narration. Click **Stop** button when you've finished speaking. If the end of the project is reached the recording will stop automatically. Your narration shows on your storyboard or timeline when you stop recording.

In Timeline mode, the narration clip will shows on a separate audio track, which can be manipulated as for any audio track. See Volume and pan on p. 159.

💡 Click the **Windows Mixer** button if you need to adjust MoviePlus volume levels from Windows.

Ripping audio CDs

There may be occasion when you may want to adopt some of your favourite audio for use in your MoviePlus project, whether as a complete song, piece, narration, or as a smaller excerpt. If located on an audio CD, MoviePlus can use ripping to capture each audio track sequentially; each track shows in your Media pane after audio ripping. By default, tracks are saved as compressed wma files.

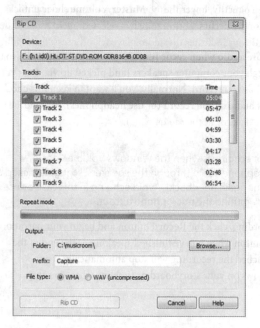

The dialog shows in-progress track-by-track digital ripping from an audio CD. Track 1 is being ripped from the audio disc in drive F (and saved in c:\musicroom\).

To rip an audio CD:

1. Click the [🎞️ Add Media...] button on the Media pane.

2. From the flyout, select the [⊙ Rip CD] button.

3. From the dialog, choose a **Device** from the drop-down list; this is the disc drive currently containing your audio CD.

4. (Optional) Use the playback controls under the track list to review tracks still on CD, e.g. use the [▶] button to play a selected track. A bar under the play control buttons indicates the audio playback progress. For ripping selected track only, uncheck unwanted tracks from the list. Otherwise, all tracks are ripped.

5. Use the **Browse...** button to specify a location that the audio files will be ripped to (they'll still show in the Media pane).

6. (Optional) Instead of a file name **Prefix** of "Capture" enter your own prefix. MoviePlus will name each captured file with an incremented number suffix.

7. (Optional) Enable the "WAV (uncompressed)" option, if you want uncompressed larger files. For wav rips, a typical 4 minute audio track will occupy about 40MB of hard drive space (typically 700MB per audio CD). Otherwise, keep the "WMA" option enabled to create smaller file sizes.

8. Click the **Rip CD** button to start ripping your checked audio tracks. A currently ripped track will show a ▲ symbol next to it; a green progress bar indicates that ripping of that track is in progress. You'll notice that ripped audio files will appear in your Media pane (in the root of your Project tab).

When you've finished capturing your audio, click the **Close** button to return to MoviePlus.

Text

Adding text

MoviePlus provides a high level of support for managing text in your project.
Typically, text within MoviePlus can be used for titles, captions, or credits.

Example	Text use
	Titles No movie is complete without initial titling to introduce the movie's name to the viewer.
	**Captions** Captions are always overlaid over an existing video or image clip, and display for that clip's duration. They are used to explain and provide context to the clip currently being displayed.
	**Credits** Credits tend to be closing credits, i.e. appearing at the end of your project, where you may want to acknowledge actors, and copyright information.

Whether you're creating titles, captions, or credits, MoviePlus offers identical
text controls for each individual text object that appears. A text object is a
single instance of text which can be modified independently of other text
objects you've added. Text controls are hosted on separate tabs on the object's
Properties pane, i.e.

- **Formatting**: Apply font type, font size, attributes, alignment, filter effects, and text styles.

- **Properties**: Control scrolling, playback and opacity.

- **Animation**: Make your titles and credits come to life—apply Blinds, Fly, Slide, Spin, and more.

- **Effects**: Include eye-catching special effects.

You'll see the above presented as separate tabs in the Properties pane whenever you've selected a text clip.

Text clips or overlays?

One of the first decisions you'll have to make with text is if your text is to be a separate text clip or an overlay over an existing clip. This decision depends on the intended text use (i.e., a title, caption or credit) as described above.

Titles

Titles are typically presented at the very beginning of your project. They tend to be a single word or at best only a few words long, but are usually shown in a large font size. MoviePlus's default behaviour is to create large text, which is ideal for titling. In fact, you'll see a default text of "My Title" when you add a Text Clip.

To add a title:

1. On the storyboard, select a clip (usually the first).
   OR
   On the timeline, set your time indicator's position.

2. Select **A Insert Text Clip** from the context toolbar.

3. Type directly into the text box selected in the Video Preview pane.

4. Drag over the text to highlight and choose a preset text style from the Properties pane (Format tab) or choose your font type, font size, text alignment, font colour, transparency, line style and whether text is to be bold, italic and/or underlined. See Formatting text on p. 176.

Captions

Captions are added in front of an existing clip either to provide a description of the underlying clip (even use one as an overlaid title at the start of your project. A typical use would be for image clips, where you could describe each photo's location, subjects in shot, etc. Whatever their use should always be succinct and informative.

To add a caption:

1. Select an existing video or image clip on your storyboard.

2. Click **A+ Add Caption** from the Video Preview pane. You'll see text added in front of the image.

3. Edit the caption as described above.

A caption can be displayed for a duration independent of the clip's duration by unchecking **Match clip duration** in the text object's Properties pane. The Duration can then be decreased, allowing the text to show only for that chosen time at the start of the clip.

In Timeline mode, the **Add Caption** button is not displayed when selecting clips. Instead, overlaid captions are possible by inserting a text clip (on a created upper track) above the video or image clip (appearing on a lower track)—the "My Title" text object is created automatically.

Credits

Credits are used to acknowledge cast and crew, as well as copyrights. They usually close a movie and tend to be presented on a neutral background (typically black). As a result, in MoviePlus it's best to present credits on their own text clip rather than as an overlay. This stops the viewer from being distracted by the underlying video clip.

A possible requirement when adding credits is the ability to display more than one frames worth of text (you may have a long list of cast, crew, and copyright information to acknowledge!). This is made possible by using **rolling credits**—the credits are made to move up, down, left, or right.

To add credits:

1. Deselect all clips on the storyboard (or move the time indicator to the end of the last clip on your timeline).

2. Select   A Insert Text Clip   from the context toolbar.

3. Type directly into the text box selected in the Video Preview pane.

4. Edit the credits as described above.

5. (Optional) To scroll overflowing credit text, set **Scrolling** in the text clip's Properties pane—choose from Up, Down, Left, or Right. Set the **Duration** of the text clip to a value which allows credits to be read comfortably (the greater the duration the slower the credits).

> To import text from other Word processing packages, cut and paste directly into the Video Preview pane. For paragraphs, you'll need to add your own line breaks to set line lengths before copying.

Adding more text

| A₊ Add more text | It's easy to add a single passage of text by clicking and
typing. However, MoviePlus can include more text via the **Add more text**
button, in addition to the initial text associated with the text clip. More text
lets you build up additional subtitles, captions, or credits. Each text object is
independent of each other and can therefore adopt its own format,
properties, animation, or effect properties. The example below shows a title
and subtitle, each possessing very different styles.

To add more text:

1. Select an existing text clip or video/image clip with overlaid text.

2. Click | A₊ Add more text | from the Video Preview pane. An additional
    text box appears which can be edited as before.

Manipulating text

You can edit, position, resize, rotate, and transform text all from within the
Video Preview pane. Manipulation is possible only once text is selected—
corner or edge control handles on the selected text's bounding box can be
used for different operations.

Selecting text

For any text clip, click on the
text you want to edit. A
bounding box appears around
the text once selected.

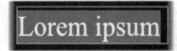

Click in the bounding box
once to select all text.

Click again for a insertion
point where you can add
additional text at that point.

To select only part of your
text, drag over part of your
text to select. Typing will
replace the selected character.

 If you need to reselect text objects, use the ⬉ **Select** button on the top
of the Video Preview pane.

Editing text

To edit text:

1. Click on text in the Video Preview pane to select the text object.

2. Click again and type to replace all text (selected in blue).
   OR
   Drag over characters or words then type to replace highlighted text only (again shown in blue).

- Use the Edit menu or keyboard shortcuts to access text editing operations such as Cut, Copy, and Paste.

- You can format text from the Properties pane (Format tab).

To add a line break:

1. Click for an insertion point at the position where you want the line to break.

2. Press the **Return** key and continue typing.

Manipulating text

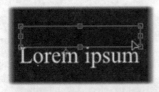

Positioning

Drag a selected text object around the pane into your ideal position.

Scaling

Scale text by dragging a corner handle (this maintains aspect ratio). Drag with **Shift** key pressed for unconstrained scaling. By default, scaling is made in relation to the opposite corner (or edge) handle. Instead, to scale from the origin point (), use the **Alt** key as you drag. Drag edge handles to stretch and shrink.

Rotating

Hover over a corner—when the cursor changes to a Rotate cursor (opposite) drag to rotate text.

To rotate about a custom origin point, press the **Ctrl** key before dragging to move the origin point (📷) to a new position.

Shearing

With the **Ctrl** key pressed, drag an edge handle to shear.

Skew

Drag a corner handle with the **Ctrl** key pressed.

Formatting text

MoviePlus lets you apply typical text formatting functions such as:

- Text formatting (font type, font size, attributes, alignment)

- Colour fill (solid and gradient) and transparency.

- Line weight and colour.

- Filter effects, such as drop shadow, glow, emboss, outlines, etc.

The **Video Preview pane** is used to select text objects (or highlighted text within) as well as add text objects. However, when used along with the Properties pane (Format tab) the above formatting is possible on selected text.

Instead of designing text styles from scratch you can adopt a text style preset from the Properties pane's Format tab instead. If needed, you can then customize text further by using the settings above the text style gallery.

To format text:

1. Select a text clip (or highlighted text) in the Video Preview pane.

2. From the Format tab, you can alter (or apply):

   - **Font** (typeface), font size, text attributes (bold, italic, underline).

   - **Paragraph** alignment (left/centre/right).

   - **Fill** (solid or gradient colour). The swatch, when clicked, lets you apply a different preset fill (or edit a fill of your own). The swatch changes to reflect the text's current colour setting.

   - **Transparency** (solid or gradient). The swatch, when clicked, lets you apply a different Transparency preset (or a edit a transparency of your own). The swatch changes to reflect the clip's current transparency setting.

- **Line**. When clicked, displays a Line Style dialog so that line weight and fill can be applied.

- **Effects.** When clicked, a dialog for applying multiple 2D and 3D filter effects is displayed. 2D effects include shadows, glow, outline, bevel, emboss, colour fill, and feathering.

Changing the line style:

- To adjust the currently selected text's line weight either drag the slider to the right or enter a point size value in the input box.

- For changes to Line fill, click the **Line fill** swatch to apply a different fill (or edit a fill of your own).

- Uncheck **Behind Fill** if you want the line fill to show over the top of your colour fill rather than behind it.

Animating text

Animation brings your text to life, creating titles, captions, or credits of great visual appeal. MoviePlus not only offers some familiar animations such as Zoom&Fade, Fly, Slide, Spin, and Explode but controls whether the animation is applied at the start or end of your text (or both). These are called **In Animations** and **Out Animations** and are key to understanding how to get the best out of your animations. As an example, the Out animation called Explode can be applied to the text clip containing the text "Animate".

With MoviePlus, animation is easy as animation presets for in and Out animations can be applied from the context toolbar or from the Galleries pane. This saves you from having to create your own animation, although you're able to customize any presets and save the resulting animation for future use.

For more than one text object in the same text clip, the same animation can be applied to all text objects in a text clip (if all objects are deselected). For individual text objects you can apply transitions independent of each other (if the text object is selected).

To apply an animation:

1. Select a text clip (or text object).

2. Click 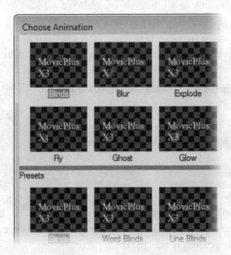 on the context toolbar.

3. From the drop-down list, pick either **Set In Animation...** or **Set Out Animation...** from the list (for a respective In or Out animation).

4. From the **Choose Animation** dialog, choose an animation category from the upper window. In the lower window, review the presets available for that category (especially their names, which indicate their intended function). Select a preset, e.g. Blinds.

5. Click **OK**.

If you've already applied an In or Out animation, repeat the above procedure to apply the complementary Out or In animation, respectively.

 For a quick way to apply an animation, open the Galleries pane, select the **Animations** button, then drag and drop a chosen preset onto your text clip (or object). A dialog lets you choose whether to add an In or Out animation.

Hover over any preset to get a preview of how your animation will look!

Once you've applied animation, you can edit animation properties in the text object's Properties. As well as being able to check which animation is applied (and it settings), you can swap out one animation for another, alter its duration, and animation-specific properties.

To edit an animation:

1. Select a text clip (or text object).

2. Choose **Edit Animations** from the ⊞ Animation ▾ drop-down list.

3. From the Animation tab on the text clip's Properties pane.

To delete an animation:

- Select a text clip (or object) with the animation applied.

- From the text clip's Properties pane (Animation tab), press ✗ Reset for the In or Out animation you want to delete.

To save your animation:

- Change the clip's name, then click the 🔲 Add to Media pane button at the top of the clip's Properties pane. The animation will appear in the Media pane's currently selected tab.

Exporting

8

Exporting

Exporting movies

There are a number of ways you can export your movie once you've edited it with MoviePlus... the project might look fantastic in your Video Preview pane, but there's likely to be an upper limit to how many people can crowd around your monitor and watch your preview, so you'll need to export your movie in a standard distributable format to allow others to share!

The considerations you'll face when deciding how to export your MoviePlus creations are the same for all video editors—the most important is "what device will the video be watched on and how am I going to deliver the video to the intended viewers?" This double-barrelled question, once answered, will help determine how you should export your movie for best results.

To export to:	You'll need to:	How to do it:
TV (with DVD) or computer	create a DVD[1]	Exporting movies via disc (see p. 184)
	create a Video CD (VCD)[1]	Exporting movies via disc (see p. 184)
iPod	Add to iTunes (for sync with iPod)	Exporting via iPod (see p. 198)
PSP	upload to PSP device[2]	Exporting via PSP (see p. 198)
YouTube	upload to YouTube[3]	Exporting via YouTube (see p. 201)
Internet	standalone file	Exporting as a file (see p. 197)

[1] *Requires DVD Writer/Rewriter or CD Writer.*
[2] *Requires a USB-connected PSP (set to USB mode).*
[3] *Requires a valid YouTube account.*

Exporting movies to disc

MoviePlus can export your project directly to disc, producing a movie which will play on your TV, computer, or other DVD-equipped device. You can create your own easy-to-navigate disc menus based on one of an impressive array of templates—all easily modifiable to suit your taste.

By default, MoviePlus will use your project settings for export, although you can switch to an Advanced mode to alter these settings specifically for export.

For DVD export, Dolby® Digital is used for audio encoding.

Disc settings

For some projects, discs can be created using settings which match your MoviePlus project settings directly (i.e., PAL DVD and their variants). However, some projects do not write transparently because their project settings (e.g., frame height, frame rate and/or pixel aspect ratio) are incompatible with MoviePlus's intended disc settings. These include not only DV projects, but custom projects possessing unusual dimensions or other characteristics. As a result, MoviePlus will determine the most appropriate disc settings from the project settings to "massage" the project into an export format suitable for disc creation. This best-matching process is done automatically. You can make alterations to the disc setting, such as the swapping the video standard or media type if necessary.

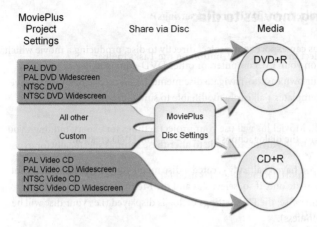

MoviePlus
Project
Settings

Share via Disc

Media

PAL DVD
PAL DVD Widescreen
NTSC DVD
NTSC DVD Widescreen

All other

Custom

MoviePlus
Disc Settings

PAL Video CD
PAL Video CD Widescreen
NTSC Video CD
NTSC Video CD Widescreen

DVD+R

CD+R

 Altering disc settings does not affect your MoviePlus project settings, but instead keeps settings solely for the disc creation process.

Several stages make up the disc creation process:

1. **Chapter point set up**. If you want a menu on your disc, chapter points define locations in your project from which menu chapter thumbnails, when clicked, will begin playing the relevant video—much the same as the initial menu shown on any Movie DVD from your local movie store. See Using markers on p. 111.

2. **Disc Setup**. To setup basic and advanced disc settings. Includes Menu Designer, a template-driven tool to easily create optional disc menus.

3. **Write Project**. To initialize and create the disc.

The user is led through each stage seamlessly, culminating in the completion of your MoviePlus project.

To create a disc (using DVD project settings):

1. Select the [Export] button on the Tasks toolbar.

2. From the dialog, choose [DVD] for DVD creation.

3. If you haven't already created a disc menu you'll be asked if you want to create one. If so, select Yes and the Menu Designer is launched. Otherwise, the Disc settings dialog is displayed (i.e., your disc will be menuless).

4. From the Disc Settings dialog, you can:

   ● Review whether a **Disc menu** is required (check or uncheck as needed), and if necessary click the **Edit...** button to edit your menu in Menu Designer (see p. 187). The preview shows your currently selected menu.

   ● Verify the video standard for your disc. Choose PAL or NTSC, and check Widescreen if required.

   ● Use the **Disc Type** drop-down list to check that your project will fit intended blank media (e.g., DVD 4.7GB). Click **Detect...** to discover your writable disc drive(s).

5. Click the **Finish** button.

6. From the Write Disc dialog, choose a write Speed and Drive where your target media is located. Your completed disc will be ejected once the process is completed.

For subsequent disc creation, caching technology is used to speed up the process.

 📄 Export For VCD creation, pick the equivalent VCD option from the
Export button on the Tasks toolbar.

 MoviePlus lets you create either an iso disc image or a DVD folder (great
for viewing DVD projects without writing to disc). For iso images, you can
write a disc from image instead of immediately committing to physical
media at a later date (see MoviePlus help).

PAL vs. NTSC video standards

Whether you choose a PAL or NTSC template should depend on whether
you intend for the video to be viewed in a PAL region or NTSC region. NTSC
is the broadcast and recording standard used mainly in North and South
American continents, plus parts of eastern Asia including Japan and South
Korea. PAL is used widely throughout Europe, Africa, the Middle East, Asia,
and Oceania.

Using Menu Designer

The Menu Designer is used for designing an optional disc menu, a
navigational aid to easily access key points in your movie called chapters. Its
user interface lets you design either your own menus from scratch or adopt a
professional-looking template preset—choose either according to the extent
of your design ability! Once your menu is complete, you can create your
DVD or VCD directly from Menu Designer.

The interface can be used to access template galleries, backgrounds, layout
options, and much more, from a single Menu Bar. When selected, each bar's
option offers a host of context-sensitive design elements appropriate to that
option chosen.

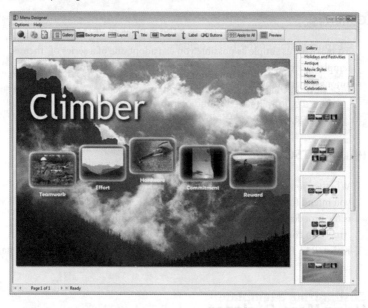

For movies with multi-page menus, typically for projects with many chapters, all pages can adopt the same design or each page can be designed differently.

Once the disc is created the menu will display when the disc is loaded, allowing easy access to important parts of your movie. When viewing the movie on computer, simply navigate via mouse; for TV, use the remote control's navigation buttons to jump between disc menu's chapters and pages.

To launch Menu Designer:

○ Click  on the Tasks toolbar.

Export You can also access Menu Designer during Disc setup (see p. 184), accessed via the **Export** button (pick the DVD or VCD option).

Galleries

To make life as simple as possible you can adopt one of a series of "themed" templates, stored in galleries such as Modern, Seasons, Funky and Moods, amongst many others.

Click the **Gallery** button to display an upper menu above a gallery of template presets for a selected menu item (as shown in example above). Choose a menu item, navigate the gallery, click a thumbnail of your chosen template, and then view your design.

Double-click on "Click to change title" and type your disc's title, then either close Menu Designer or, more typically, customize your template further.

Customizing a template

The Background, Layout, Title, Thumbnails, Buttons, and Labels buttons can all be used to modify your chosen template. By clicking any one of these options along the top bar the user interface refreshes to display an appropriate menu and accompanying gallery on the right-hand side of the Menu Designer workspace. For example, if you click Title, then a text-related menu will be shown above a gallery of title presets. Try it out by clicking on each button on the Menu Bar!

Click the button to display an upper menu of background types above a series of gallery thumbnails for the selected menu item. You can choose from a gallery of solid or gradient colours, or from a range of artistic background images.

To import your own image or video for use as a background, click **My Image or Video**, then click the **Add** button. From the Open dialog, choose a media file to add to the background gallery—click the media file to apply it as a background.

To animate a movie background, click **Page Setup** on the Menu Bar, and check **Animate Background**.

Pick an accompanying layout which will house thumbnails for all chapters, either on a single or multiple pages. Thumbnails are arranged in rows, columns or in more artistic patterns. For example, a page layout with eight thumbnails would match perfectly with a movie with eight chapters.

If you choose a layout option with less chapter thumbnails than the number of chapters in your project you automatically create a multi-page disc menu. For example, a "4 Per Page" layout would create a two-page disc menu for a MoviePlus project with 8 chapters.

If you want to change the attributes of your current title, click this button. The gallery will show a range of preset titles with various effects applied—some relatively modest, some downright flashy! Select a preset closest to the one you want to use. The titling will update on your main page to reflect the change.

If you want to then edit your title, use the menu to change the Font, Effects, Colour and crop of all your title characters.

The Menu Designer supports in-place text editing, which means direct editing of title text is possible. Either click on the title and type to replace the title text or type at a insertion point to add more text. You can perform all the common text editing functions such as copy (Ctrl+C), paste (Ctrl+V), and delete; you can also add a soft carriage return with Ctrl-Return.

Select this button then choose a category (e.g., Ellipse, Star, Diamond, amongst others) from the upper menu then pick a preset from the lower gallery—a whole range of thumbnail shapes and styles are available. Once applied, change the thumbnail style from the upper menu with respect to border effects (e.g., shadows), colour, and opacity.

Chapter thumbnail labels can be modified as described above for Titles. Note that the change affects all labels and not an individual label. In-place text editing is supported.

For VCD menus, the labels will be prefixed with a number, which can be pressed from your remote control.

Navigation buttons are used to navigate between multi-page disc menus. You can swap out the current buttons, especially if a colour clash occurs with your background (preset or imported). Click the button to reveal a gallery of buttons. Pick a button style, then select your chosen button colour from the menu above the button gallery.

For multi-page menus, changes are made across all pages by default. If the button is disabled, changes are made to the current page only.

Click this button to view how your project will look like on your TV without the need to create a disc. Preview, adjust your page design, then preview again until your menu is to your satisfaction. Use the accompanying buttons to simulate your DVD player's remote control for testing purposes.

Editing chapter properties

When you launch Menu Designer, you'll see either:

- a single thumbnail called "My Movie" appear in your menu workspace. This occurs if you haven't inserted chapter points on your timeline. To add chapter points, see Using markers on p. 111 for more information. OR

- If you have inserted chapter points onto your storyboard or timeline (as part of video editing), a series of thumbnails are shown which represent the chapter at which you added a chapter point.

Once chapters are present, their properties can be edited or viewed, i.e. you can:

- preview the content of each chapter by playback.

- zoom in/out of individual frames to inspect the chapter.

- swap to a different thumbnail (taken directly from the frame at the chapter point position), e.g. a frame which typifies a chapter much more than any other.

○ change the chapter name, i.e. the label shown next to the thumbnail.

○ change chapter end action, i.e. the action expected once the chapter has finished playing in your DVD player. The usual action is to **Progress to next chapter**, but it is also possible to **Return to title page**.

To view chapters:

○ Double-click a chapter thumbnail in the menu workspace.

In the Chapter Properties dialog, the video frames displayed for a chapter are those spanning between the selected and the next chapter point on the timeline (if no chapter point exists after the current one the remainder of the movie is shown).

The following navigation controls assist with the inspection, viewing and editing of the chapter.

○ On the **Seek** bar you can drag your Current time indicator (a vertical line which represents your current location) to any point in the video (between the current and the next chapter point).

○ The [icon] **Go to Start** or [icon] **Go to End** button lets you send your Current time indicator to the start or end of your chapter, respectively.

○ Use the [icon] **Previous Frame** and [icon] **Next Frame** buttons to fine tuning the position of the Current time indicator.

○ Click the [icon] **Play** button to start previewing the video between chapter points. The preview will begin from your current time indicator position.

● Use the 🔍 **Zoom In** and 🔍 **Zoom Out** buttons to locate specific frames more easily. For longer chapters, picking the correct frame may be more difficult as the entire chapter is made to fit the window.

To use a different frame as thumbnail:

● In Chapter properties, use the navigation controls to navigate then pick the right frame. Once you're happy with the thumbnail shown in the preview window, click the **Jump to Caret** button (this aligns the red **Image** indicator under the Current time indicator position). On exit, this thumbnail will now be shown to represent your chapter.

OR

● Drag the red indicator, which realigns then synchronizes the Current time indicator to it. This automatic alignment provides a simple method for alternative thumbnail selection (avoiding the Jump to Caret operation).

Changing the thumbnail picture does not affect the chapter point positions on the timeline. However, moving chapter points on the timeline will reposition your modified thumbnail, so remember to always check thumbnails are correctly set.

To rename your chapter:

● In Chapter properties, enter a new **Name** (or edit the existing name).

Disc options

The 💿 **Disc Options** button on the Menu Bar (or Options menu), when clicked, shows a dialog which lets you play the initial chapter before showing the disc menu. Optionally, all the thumbnails can be hidden with the **Show chapter thumbnails** option.

Setting background music

By default, no background music is played when your disc menu is displayed on your TV/PC screen. However, it's often a nice finishing touch to complement your menu design with supporting audio—use it for instructional reasons or to simply play background music. The audio stream of a video file can also be used as a background music.

> If you've used a background video on your page, you can use its audio as a menu soundtrack.

The same music can be applied to all pages or you can apply different music to the current page only.

To enable background music:

1. Click the **Page Setup** button on the Menu Bar.

2. From the dialog, pick an option from the **Music** section. Either:

   ○ For music from a **saved audio or video file:**
     Click the second radio button, and either type the path to the media file or click the **Browse** button to navigate to the file. For the latter, navigate and select a media file (video file must contain audio) from the dialog. Common Audio files such as .MP3, .WAV, and .WMA are supported, as well as video files such as .AVI, .MPG, .MOV, .WMV and .ASF.
     OR

   ○ For music from the **page's background video**:
     Enable the **Use soundtrack from background video** button. You must have previously set a video as the Custom Background from the same dialog.

3. Click **OK**.

Writing project

The Menu Bar hosts a [button icon] button which displays a drop-down menu with the following options:

- Write DVD. Displays disc settings. Once set, you can initiate the physical DVD writing process (via a Write Disc dialog).
  OR

- Write VCD. As for Write DVD, but the VCD writing process is used instead.

Animating your menu

If your menu needs some extra visual appeal it's possible to animate your thumbnails or background, or both. This will automatically play movie chapters within their thumbnail preview, or play any currently configured video background.

To animate thumbnails and/or video backgrounds:

- In [icon] **Page Setup**, check either **Animate Thumbnails** or **Animate Background**, or both. A slider sets the time the thumbnails or background will animate for before the animation loops and plays again.

Closing Menu Designer

- Choose **Exit Menu Designer** in the Options menu or click the [X icon] **Close** button. You will be prompted to save your project if it is currently unsaved. Your updated template will be shown by default the next time you load the Menu Designer.

Exporting as a file

There are many different reasons for exporting your movie as a file, but they all share the need or wish to get other people viewing your video masterpiece. Crowds around your own computer screen using the MoviePlus Video Preview pane to watch your video just aren't practical! Whether your driving force is to attain a small file size to share a little video by email or over the Internet, MoviePlus can export your projects in a suitable file format to help you achieve your goal.

To export as a file:

1. Select the [Export] button on the Tasks toolbar.

2. From the dialog, choose [File].

3. Select your chosen file type from the list according to intended use, then click **Next>**.

4. From the Export Settings dialog, several options are available:

   ● (Optional) Select a preset export template (choose from Normal or Widescreen templates). Click **Customize...** to create your own export template if necessary.

   ● (Optional) Change render quality (between **Draft** and **Best** quality). Set Draft if you're testing your export. The **Render Quality** setting controls the level of video and audio processing carried out during export—affecting the visual quality of effects and transitions applied to clips in your project. A **Best** render quality means a longer export time compared to **Draft,** but this gives high-quality effects and transitions. To save time, use the latter when testing your export.

  ○ (Optional; timeline mode only) (Optional; timeline mode only) If
     you're exporting just part of your project, the **Export selected
     range** option can be checked to limit the export; you need to
     place selection markers on your timeline first.

5. Click **Finish**.

6. To save the file, locate a target folder and specify a name for your file
   in the **File name** box, then click the **Save** button. Your project will
   then be composed and converted into the specified format and you
   will be shown a progress bar during this process.

7. On completion, the file can be opened with the **Open** button (to play
   the resulting video in your default media player software), you can
   explore the file's folder with **Open Folder** or just **Close** the dialog and
   return to MoviePlus.

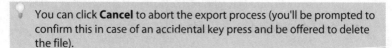

You can click **Cancel** to abort the export process (you'll be prompted to
confirm this in case of an accidental key press and be offered to delete
the file).

Exporting to iPod/PSP

As more and more entertainment platforms vie for worldwide dominance,
the more the opportunity exists to share your movies on a range of modern
devices. Two of the most successful platforms are the Apple iPod (for music
and video) and the Sony PSP (gaming, music and video).

MoviePlus makes sharing with such devices straightforward, with respective
exporting to iTunes and uploading to PSP possible.

iPod

Exporting your movie via a video-capable Apple iPods is carried out in two
stages—exporting the movie to iTunes and subsequently syncing the movie
to your iPod. MoviePlus takes care of the first stage, but you'll need to sync
your movie to iPod as you would for any other movie file.

To export to iPod:

1. Select the button on the Tasks toolbar.

2. From the dialog, choose **iPod/PSP**.

3. From the iPod/PSP dialog, select device type, standard, and quality setting as follows:

   - Pick your target device. Enable **iPod** for Apple iPods.

   - Choose your video standard: **PAL** for Europe, Africa, the Middle East, most of Asia, and Oceania; **NTSC** for North and South American continents, plus parts of eastern Asia including Japan and South Korea.

   - Select a video **Quality**. For testing, **Low** quality will create a lower quality movie by reducing the Video bit rate on export.

   - Uncheck the **Add exported file to iTunes** option if you just want to export the movie file, rather than add the file to iTunes library automatically. The option changes depending on whether iPod or PSP is enabled as an option.

4. From the **Save As** dialog, locate a target folder and specify a name for your mp4 video file in the **File name** box, then click the **Save** button. Your project will then be composed and converted into the specified format; you will be shown a progress bar during this process.

> You can click **Cancel** to abort the export process (you'll be prompted to confirm this in case of an accidental key press and be offered to delete the file).

5. On completion, the file can be opened with the **Open** button (to play the resulting video in your default media player software) or you can explore the file's folder with Open **Folder** (or just **Close** the dialog and return to MoviePlus).

6. Click **Continue** to launch iTunes automatically. Your movie will already be added to your iTunes library (under Movies).

The next time you connect your iPod to your computer your movie will synchronize with the iPod.

via PSP

If you own a Sony PSP, you can export your movie easily. In USB mode, your PSP is seen as any other removable storage device—as such your movie is uploaded onto the device with the minimum of fuss.

 To upload, your PSP **must** be in USB mode.

To export to PSP:

1. As for exporting via iPod (above) but instead of the **Device Type** being iPod choose **PSP**. Instead of clicking **Finish** to save to a file, you can upload to the connected device directly if **Upload exported file to PSP** remains checked (otherwise only the movie is exported). Click **Next>**.

2. From the **Upload to PSP** dialog, give the movie a title and select the PSP device from the drop-down menu. This should show the PSP as a removable storage device, i.e.

    Select a PSP to upload to:

    H: (Sony PSP USB Device)

3. (Optional) Check **Keep a local copy...** to save the exported movie for use again (leads to quicker exports for unchanged projects).

4. Click **Finish**. The project will then be composed and converted into the specified format and you will be shown a progress bar during this process.

You can click **Cancel** to abort the export process (you'll be prompted to confirm this in case of an accidental key press and be offered to delete the file).

5. Click **Continue** to upload the local movie up to the PSP.

Exporting to YouTube

You may have been aware of the mass popularity of video hosting sites, notably YouTube, in recent years. Placing a movie on YouTube means that you can share a short movie worldwide without writing to media or uploading to your own web site. The two-stage process involves exporting a file optimized for upload (i.e., wmv) then uploading the file to the YouTube website.

A working YouTube login is required to upload your movie. If you don't have a login, visit www.youtube.com and register!

To export to YouTube:

1. Select the 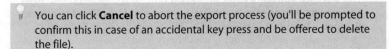 button on the Tasks toolbar.

2. From the dialog, choose .

3. From the Export Settings dialog, select a video **Quality**. For testing, **Low** quality will create a lower quality movie by reducing the Video bit rate on export. Click **Next>**.

4. From the **Save As** dialog, locate a target folder and specify a name for your wmv video file in the **File name** box, then click the **Save** button.

Your project will then be composed and converted into the specified format and you will be shown a progress bar during this process.

> You can click **Cancel** to abort the export process (you'll be prompted to confirm this in case of an accidental key press and be offered to delete the file).

5. On completion, the file can be opened with the **Open** button to check before YouTube upload (this plays your video in your default media player software) or you can explore the file's folder with **Open Folder** (or just **Close** the dialog and return to MoviePlus).

6. Click **Continue** to launch the YouTube Upload dialog. Add your YouTube login details (UserID and Password), movie **Title** and **Description**, a YouTube Video **Category**, and some keywords (**Tags**) for users to search for.

Instead, you can upload by using valid Google account details (but you'll still need a valid YouTube UserID also).

7. Click **Finish** to begin the file upload. A progress bar is shown during upload.

Archiving to camcorder (Print to Tape)

The DV or HDV video format is used extensively by digital tape-based camcorders, so many video clips exist in this format before being edited. Although MoviePlus can export your project to many types of video format, you can choose to either export your project to a connected camcorder or to a file for writing to a camcorder at a later date. Either way, this is an important feature if you want to archive your completed movie to tape.

Exporting directly to your camcorder is a two-step process as MoviePlus first creates a file before transferring it to your camcorder. However, if you already have an exported file that you want to archive you can initiate the second step by using the **Write file to DV/HDV Camcorder...** on the Tools menu, choosing the correct file type from the resulting dialog's file type drop-down list, then selecting the target file.

To write to DV or HDV camcorder (also called print to tape):

1. Select the ⟦ Export ⟧ button on the Tasks toolbar.

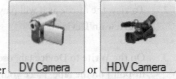

2. From the dialog, choose either ⟦ DV Camera ⟧ or ⟦ HDV Camera ⟧ for DV or HDV camcorders, respectively.

3. Check that your DV or HDV template from the **Export Settings** list is correct. If not, choose a different setting. For information about choosing PAL or NTSC menu options, please see NTSC vs. PAL on p. 187.

4. (Optional) Change render quality (between **Draft** and **Best** quality). Set Draft if you're testing your export. The **Render Quality** setting controls the level of video and audio processing carried out during export—affecting the visual quality of effects and transitions applied to clips in your project. A **Best** render quality means a longer export time

compared to **Draft,** but this gives high-quality effects and transitions. To save time, use the latter when testing.

5. (Optional) Uncheck **Keep export file**, to always recreate the export file (avoiding file caching).

6. Click **Finish**.

7. To save the file, locate a target folder and specify a name for your avi (for DV) or m2t file (for HDV) in the **File name** box, then click the **Save** button. Your project will then be composed and converted into the specified format and you will be shown a progress bar during this process.

> Once the first stage of exporting is complete, you'll need to have your camcorder connected and set to Record mode before continuing.

Step two

1. Click the Export Complete dialog's **Continue** button.

2. To view the movie as it will play back on your camcorder, select the **Preview on Device** tab.

3. On the **Write to Device** tab, use the control buttons to locate a suitable in-point on the tape. Place your camcorder in Stop mode.

4. Adjust the **Write Delay** value if necessary to insert a timed pause before MoviePlus begins feeding data to the camcorder. The target camcorder may be digital, but it's also mechanical and different transport mechanisms have different response times. A few tests will establish exactly how long your camcorder takes to start recording once it's activated. (When in doubt, it's better to set the delay slightly too long than too short.)

5. To begin recording, click **Write to Device**.

Index